OPENING SCIENCE FOR ALL:
A Continuing Quest

Cecily Cannan Selby

Publisher's Information

EBookBakery Books

ISBN: 978-1-938517-82-2
Author contact: cecily.selby@gmail.com

Front cover images: Woods Hole, MA, artist and potter Joan Lederman glazes bowls with deep-sea ocean sediments and then fires them at high temperatures, creating imagery, shown on the front cover, that evokes the partnership between humans and nature and the power discussed in this book of questions that incorporate diverse modes of inquiry.

DEDICATION

With pride, admiration and unbounded love, I dedicate this story of my life and loves to my grandchildren, Luke, Thomas, Catherine, Alexandra and Christina Selby. Sharing the delights and accomplishments of their early years has been the highest privilege of my life, enabling me to imagine all the delights and satisfactions they will open up for themselves in their years to come.

TABLE OF CONTENTS

ACKNOWLEDGMENTS

Opening Science For All acknowledges with enduring thanks and appreciation the many precious friends, colleagues and family members with whom I developed the ideas and the passion that fed this book. And always, the unflagging support of my sons Norman, Bill and Russell, were where I could turn for the support, shared experiences and love essential to continuing this task, new and difficult for me.

My parents, with their love of good ideas, good words, and care and consideration of others, set the direction for my lifetime of choices. My father's love of science opened doors for me to science as an exciting and friendly place in which to satisfy my curiosity, while his care and support for his student Jonas Salk introduced me to the gratifications of teaching and learning.

Phillip Frank's college teaching about physics and philosophy germinated my intellectual growth, particularly in physics and regarding its influence on society. During my years exploring the structure of biological cells, Keith Porter and George Palade's generosity in sharing their experiments and ideas in biology fed my thinking and my work for decades. Gerald Holton's writings particularly enriched my years of teaching NYU graduate courses, including Science and Human Values, The Scientific Enterprise, and Science in Historical Perspective. Working with the cognitive and computer explorations of Seymour Papert was also an enduring influence and privilege. My former students, Diane Sherlock at Lenox School, and Maura Flannery, Paul Jablon and Janice Koch at NYU, are remembered with great fondness and admiration for their own research and contributions to my thinking. Pamela Fraser-Abder's career at NYU, following mine, became a source of continuing learning and friendships. Especially fond memories remain with colleagues at the Lenox School, the North Carolina School of Science and Mathematics, the Radcliffe Institute, NYU and the New York Hall of Science. In each place, and over time, we developed policies and practices that did open science to everyone we reached!

From the time this book was just an idea in my head, a personal friend, Michaela Walsh, has been a faithful advocate, always insisting I not give up on writing it. As the book began to take shape, my Woods Hole friend, anthropologist and writer Jeanne Guillemin, consulted generously with her time and professional talent. During the last years of writing and editing, Steve Uzzo of the New York Hall of Science was a source of knowledge, and, in Woods Hole, Debora Wells provided thoughtful assistance. The faithful secretarial support and good company of Regine Rossi and Margo Cruz was invaluable throughout. Special gratitude goes to the extensive editing skills and judgment of Vicky Cullen and the publishing expertise of Michael Grossman, who together brought the book across the finish line. Above all, I thank my husband, James S. ("Spike") Coles, who dearly wanted me to write this book and would so have loved to see it to come to pass.

∽

There is also a place for which I am enduringly grateful: Woods Hole, Cape Cod, Massachusetts. It is I where I both grew up and chose to retire, and where I absorbed the values, tastes, and interests that I like most in myself. I consider it my "hometown." One of the many gifts of this beautiful and lively place has been friendship with ceramic artist Joan Lederman, whose work graces the front cover of this book. Admiring her work, and sharing my work with her, we often compared her aesthetic inquiries into the material nature of our cosmos with my scientific inquiries into the life within it. Such comparisons reveal both similarities between the processes of artistic and scientific inquiries and vast differences between how they frame questions and what they choose to pay attention to. My gratitude for Joan's artistic partnership in contributing the exquisite beauty of her images goes beyond words. While I know readers will enjoy the beauty and excitement of Joan's images from nature, I hope they will also learn why and how such original discoveries must and can be open to all.

Introduction

Now these people, while provided with a good intelligence, yet, because they cannot understand what is written [in books], retain through life the idea that those big folios contain matters beyond their capacity which will forever remain closed to them; whereas I want them to realize that nature, as she has given them eyes to see her works, has given them a brain apt to grasp and understand them.

—Galileo Galilei, 15th Century

In this book I write about spending a wonderful life with science and scientists, always regretting, as Galileo did long ago, that the delights science was bringing me were not open to everyone. These regrets began in my earliest years when I thought that science was friendly and fun, but my classmates did not. That our opinions differed was easy to understand. Mine came from growing up in a science-friendly home and community, while my classmates had absorbed widespread notions that science is good for boys but difficult and boring for girls. Following Galileo, I also learned that most people still believe science is "beyond their capacity." Distressed by what I thought they were missing, I determined that, in my years ahead, I must find out how to open science not just to classmates, but to everyone.

But first, I needed to learn more about science myself and happily did so in study and research along an academic track. Working in laboratories and libraries with other scientists, we shared and were unified by our common understanding of the science we were practicing and analyzing every day. When, however, after marriage and the birth of three sons, I moved my work to classrooms, offices and boardrooms, I found little agreement and much misinformation about what science is and what scientists do. Scientists are very successful at explaining how the world works, but are, apparently, less successful in explaining how science itself works! I was surprised to discover that, in teaching and media communications, science's products get wide attention but the processes that create these products do not. Time and again, I observed misperceptions to be prime culprits in closing science to the public.

Seeking to replace misperceptions with valid descriptions, I searched my own research experiences and the writings of contemporary scientists. What I found is reviewed and commented upon in my last chapter. All are agreed that science is an Inquiry, not a Method: an inquiry whose answers must be verified and agreed upon by others using the same criteria for validity. Once agreed upon, science's answers are open to everyone, becoming common knowledge, useful to all.

The stories I tell in this book highlight how an inquirer's personal perspectives, tastes and styles can remain alive and recognizable throughout a scientific inquiry. Thus, science, like all modes of human inquiry, should be recognized, and taught, as personal inquiry. Nature can only respond to the questions we ask of it in the way the questions are asked. It replies more broadly to broadly framed questions, and more narrowly to narrowly framed questions. Having the same question asked in different ways by different people with different perspectives adds scope and accuracy to nature's answers. Understanding this reality provides lasting evidence that different participants (including women and other underserved minorities) add value to any investigation. I conclude my stories with the "discovery" that science and its inquiry are both personal and democratic. Scientific inquiry, as all inquiry, welcomes diversity among participants and requires diversity for its successes.

My story is a woman's story as it describes how a wife, mother and scientist chose to join, and then found ways to thrive in, workplaces that support positive family/work relationships. It is an optimistic story that promotes the "open science" so essential today to advancing "open societies." And it highlights how asking and answering scientific questions can assist and support inquiries in the arts and humanities—and politics—in collaborations so fruitful today.

This memoir has messages for all audiences. For parents, I describe the culture and activities that accompany their children's science studies. For educators, I describe projects that, during my lifetime, successfully advanced the content, pedagogy, effectiveness and enjoyment of science teaching and learning. And, I hope it helps bring to all students a broader and deeper awareness of the pleasures, power, usefulness and fun that science's way of framing questions and seeking answers can add to everyday as well as to professional life. A useful understanding of scientific inquiry also opens a gateway to the innovative modes of inquiry offered in new STEM (science, technology, engineering and mathematics) fields such as computer science, data science and artificial intelligence.

Concluding this introduction, I recall Einstein's well-chosen words: "The whole of science is nothing more than a refinement of everyday thinking." Confident that Galileo would have agreed, I suggest that science will be open to all when all also agree.

Cecily Cannan Selby

Synopsis

Opening Science For All:
A Continuing Quest

I first met science at "my father's knee," and in Woods Hole, a small village on Cape Cod where my parents and I spent our summers. Woods Hole is a lively seaside community, home to five scientific institutions, where science is widely spoken, studied and enjoyed, often together with the arts and humanities. There, at home and on the beach, I was fascinated by scientists' playfulness with ideas and their ways of asking and answering questions, and found them irresistible. I also noticed that what boys and men did looked much more interesting than what girls and women could do. When I discovered at school that my classmates thought science dull, difficult and accessible only to boys "good at math," my lifelong ambition to learn more about science so that I could help open its doors to others was born.

My memoir opens with my transition from a somewhat iconoclastic girlhood (not bothered that boys were supposed to be better at math and science) to a concentration in physics as an undergraduate at Radcliffe, and then on to a 1950 doctorate, at age 23, in physical biology at MIT. Often the only woman in the classroom, breaking glass ceilings in nonprofit organizations and corporate boardrooms became a lifelong habit. While sad not to be working with more women, I felt lucky to be a pioneer in exploring new territories and asking new questions. A sense of adventure continued to characterize my life and my passion for science.

My first intellectual adventures came while an undergraduate, in Harvard's physics and philosophy classes, but my attention soon moved from the tiniest of particles in the physical world to living cells in the biological world. Studying for a Ph.D. at MIT, I learned how to conduct a scientific investigation, manage an experiment and use the new tool of X-ray diffraction. During the next ten happy and productive post-doctorate years as a research scientist at the Sloan-Kettering Institute and Cornell Medical School in New York, I used another new, path-breaking tool: electron microscopy. As an independent scientist, studying the structures within normal and cancer cells, I relished the individual initiative and collaborative skills of problem-solving that make a scientist's day, and the special delight of seeing my discoveries published in scientific journals for worldwide distribution. I well knew that the scientific evidence I was seeking must be "objective": transparent, verifiable and falsifiable. But, in my work and in that of others, I soon recognized legitimate roles for subjectivity within inquiry and experimentation. Scientists' autobiographies often describe how their personalities, tastes and styles influence their work. I was first attracted to science by the personalities and cultural breadth of scientists I met in childhood. Later, I identified their thinking as a blend of the personal, rational, subjective and objective, a source of the creative thinking essential to good science and worthwhile discoveries.

But, other even stronger influences began to affect my life. After my marriage to a physician (1950) and the births of our three sons, my delight in cancer research gave way to a greater need and desire to have more time to care for my husband and children. I resigned from the medical school faculty and moved to a busy life at home in the house we had bought nearby. To add needed income to our family budget, and to explore science education, I accepted a part-time position teaching science at the nearby Lenox School for girls. When this led to an appointment as the school's headmistress, my career as an educator began. Family-work conflicts were resolved. Happy years with my growing sons followed with our work and family life well mixed. As I later recognized, changing workplaces also added value to my own life and to new workplaces that were to come.

Now that I was responsible for twelve grades of school for girls, I learned how little of the science I knew and loved could be found in school curricula. School teaching emphasized what scientists had learned rather than how they learned. The focus was on the usefulness of its products, not its processes. With teachers' help, I enriched and amplified our science courses so that students and parents soon agreed that learning science was not just for boys and mathematical "nerds." And, my own understanding of the benefits of science education blossomed when I noticed how readily the skills developed managing laboratory experiments transferred to managing people and institutions. "Management skills" were soon added to my list of benefits of science study.

The 1970s brought new attention and mandates to women's advancement in professions, and with it, unexpected invitations for me to join corporate and nonprofit management, often as the first, or only, female CEO or board member. As National Executive Director of Girls Scouts of the U.S.A., a member of Fortune 500 corporate boards, CEO of a Washington, DC, NGO and a university trustee, I had another surprise: I was not just a minority in gender, but, even more significantly, in science and technological literacy. Such literacy had not yet been recognized as helpful to making policy and solving societal problems. Science literacy for responsible adults also immediately joined my list of desired educational objectives. More bad news arrived when I learned that, in Washington, "education" meant "lobbying," not teaching and learning. But, I did learn about the excellent science and technology instruction available in Girl Scouts of the U.S.A. in their informal "hands-on" activities.

These years spent away from science made me wiser and even more committed to promoting science and technological literacy. I welcomed an invitation to help create the North Carolina School for Science and Mathematics, our nation's first tuition-free boarding school for gifted high school students located in Durham, North Carolina. Founded and enthusiastically supported by North Carolina's governor, Jim Hunt, diversity among students and faculty and strong science and technology education were, and remain, the school's mission. This school continues to be successful in its outreach to diverse students and in opening science for them and the community. Working closely with faculty, local community leaders and the governor in designing and operating this new educational enterprise, I needed and used virtually all I had yet learned.

But soon, new horizons awaited me back in New York. In 1981, I returned home to remarry and start a new life with a husband whose career also focused on science, education and management. Immediately a devoted partner in my work, he shared delight in my appointment in 1982 as co-chair of the National Science Foundation's (NSF's) first commission to evaluate the status and needs of the nation's K-12 science, mathematics and technology education. After eighteen months of Commission workshops and interviews across the U.S., we assessed what we had learned and built recommendations for national action. Our final report to the nation in 1983 declared, for the first time in the U.S., that science education must be available to all students. We wrote "All students need a firm grounding in mathematics, science and technology," and "the 'basics' of the 21st century....[must] include communication and higher problem-solving skills, and scientific and technological literacy." Incorporating the extensive data we had collected, our report made clear that advancing science education requires more and better teacher education, technology education and attention to lifelong learning. These recommendations framed NSF's commitment of resources to science, technology and education for decades to come.

Concluding that enhanced and enriched teacher education should be a top priority for the nation, I eagerly accepted an appointment as Professor of Science Education at New York University. Teaching graduate courses to New York City science teachers was a delight, personally and professionally, and helped me consolidate my understanding of what teachers need and want to meet the nation's goals in science education.

More than a decade later, I was invited to attend the 1995 United Nations Conference on Women in Science and Technology in Beijing, China. There, it was thrilling to hear a delegate from Nigeria stand up at a plenary session to declare, "Our girls and our women need education in science and technology as much as our boys and men." A new era with science open to all was dawning. But, as my years away from the laboratory had shown me, prevalent misperceptions about science continued to block full popular engagement with science—still considered by many to be too complex or too boring.

Slowly but surely I concluded that outdated and misinformed definitions for science blocked paths to the science literacy we were seeking for all. To reach this objective, we need public perceptions of what science is and what scientists do that support trust and identify science as diverse, accessible, personal, open, and valuable to all.

Following retirement from academic positions and the death of my husband in 1996, I was invited, as a Teaching Fellow at Harvard's Radcliffe Institute, to develop a program: Gender, Science, and Society. This appointment gave me precious time and resources to develop evidence and arguments for changing axioms guiding communication about science. Researching the writings of contemporary scholars, I found all agreed that science is an inquiry, not a method, and that, as in all other modes of human inquiry, the inquirer's personal characteristics and perspectives can influence the inquiry. Agreement on this point prompts agreement that diversity among those engaged in practicing science adds value to its outcomes. Each mode of human inquiry is distinguished by the evidence each pays attention to. Science's contribution to all human inquiry is its insistence on verifiable evidence on which everyone can agree. Since scientific evidence can be shared, it becomes useful to all.

My book concludes with these messages from my later years: Scientific modes of inquiry, science's way of asking and seeking to answer questions, are accessible and can be useful to all humanity. Access to science literacy is through scientific inquiry, a mode of human inquiry that is personal, democratic and a part of all of us. It needs and deserves equal opportunity to participate with all other modes of human inquiry in human and societal development.

Chapter Outlines

CHAPTER ONE: A New Spirit

Our work can seem like a pleasant hobby to us, it can sustain a sense of wonder, and bring us joy and fulfillment.
—*Henry Stommel, Oceanographer, 1989*

After being welcomed in 1927 as a "New Spirit" into an open-minded Theosophist-run London lying-in hospital, I moved to New York City with my biochemist father and classicist mother when I was three. My introduction to science was at home and during summers in Woods Hole, a Cape Cod community where no one was scared of science and women scientists were not an oddity. I grew up thinking that science was friendly and fun for everyone. Music and the arts also flourished there, and my mother introduced me to piano playing, singing and dancing, but it was science's way of satisfying curiosity that I found irresistible. I read in the library where Rachel Carson and Jonas Salk (my father's student at New York University's Medical School) had also read, and decided that I liked the things that boys and men did better than what girls and women did. Yet I was sad and distressed when I found that, in my schools and in college, science was not considered friendly or interesting for everyone. I well remember my three child-hood wishes: for a library, horn-rimmed glasses and an older brother.

CHAPTER TWO: A Female Harvard in Wartime

The art of research is that of making a problem soluable by finding out ways of getting at it.
—*Peter Medawar, Biologist, 1979*

I entered Radcliffe/Harvard in 1943, quite "different" from my classmates: British, studying science and, thanks to my English and Canadian boarding schools, a sophomore, two years younger than most classmates. Still, I soon fit happily into class and school activities. Already attracted to physics and philosophy, and aware that physics was helping to win the war, I chose physics for my undergraduate major. Knowing that my father was busy with wartime science policies, government became my minor study, and led to my representing Radcliffe at the first meeting of the United World Federalists. During these wartime years, Army and Navy officers in training filled Harvard dormitories and my physics and math classes, where I was often the only female. In an editorial I was asked to write for *The Radcliffe News* following the Hiroshima bombing, I expressed concern that technology's burgeoning usefulness would lead it to dominate our way of life. My citation, upon election as a junior member of Sigma Xi (science's Phi Beta Kappa) said that I had "future research potential," and this suggested to me an obligation to continue in science. At our 1946 graduation, my class joined the post-war world, having earned the first Radcliffe diplomas signed by Harvard's president.

CHAPTER THREE: A Minority at MIT

> *Scientific methodology today is based on generating hypotheses and testing them to see if they can be falsified; this methodology is what distinguishes science from other fields of human endeavor.*
> —U.S. SUPREME COURT, 1993, QUOTING SIR KARL POPPER

A German wartime film showing high magnification images of living cells dividing shifted my curiosity from physics' tiny particles to biology's small living cells. Learning that a new department of physical biology at MIT was initiating the application of physics and its tools to biology, I applied for admission. Although I had not studied biology in school or college, my math and physics background qualified me for the program, so I became one of a tiny female minority at MIT, entirely happy to be there and doing what the boys were doing. My department maintained an informal, bias-free and friendly culture with which it was leading the new era of molecular and physical biology. From my Ph.D. professor, I learned the X-ray diffraction techniques being used at the same time in Cambridge, England, to obtain the successful molecular model of DNA, and applied it to my study of the molecular structure of the clam adductor muscle. This work was subsequently published in *Nature* as "The 'Lotmar-Picken' X-Ray

Diffraction Diagram of Muscle." Informal meetings and contacts with distinguished international scientists visiting our department (Erwin Schrödinger, J.D. Bernal, and Chandrasekhar V. Raman) stimulated my thinking and foreshadowed lifelong delight with the philosophical and humanistic minds of great scientists.

CHAPTER FOUR: From Laboratories to Home

Others (women) in love with their science and doing great work leave because of inhospitable workplaces and prejudice . . . in the evaluation of their talent.

—NANCY HOPKINS, MIT,
STUDY ON WOMEN FACULTY IN SCIENCE, 1999

In 1950, with my new MIT Ph.D., I was working at the Sloan-Kettering Institute in New York, where I met my future husband, Henry M. "Hank" Selby, MD. Our marriage a year later happily fulfilled my personal life while electron microscopy redirected my professional life. My white lab coat covered three pregnancies as our first son was born in 1952, a second in 1954, and our last in 1955. My mother, newly widowed, became a very helpful and beloved grandmother, while Scandinavian "mothers' helpers" helped with childcare. My work was supported by generous post-war funding for cancer research, and my electron microscope studies of skin, muscle and cancer cells were published in professional journals. Sharing a large medical community with my husband, and lunching often in the Doctors' Dining Room, I enjoyed belonging to a "club" of scientists and doctors whose shared understanding of scientific inquiry enabled discussion of each other's work, despite differences in our technical vocabularies. We could share our questions and how we chose to answer them. Appointed an instructor at Weill Cornell's Medical College, I taught and advised medical students. Encouraged by faculty there, and at Sloan-Kettering, I continued to enjoy a happy integration of home and workplace. However, as needs at home escalated, my resignation from teaching and research followed.

CHAPTER FIVE: Girls' Schooling and Scouting

Science promotes critical inquiry, curiosity and democracy.
Through its focus on evidence and honesty, science provides
a way to call the bluff of those who would lie to us.
—RAMPELE MANPHELA, VICE CHANCELLOR,
UNIVERSITY OF CAPE TOWN, 1999

While at home with my sons, an unexpected phone call brought an invitation to consider a part-time job teaching science at the Lenox School, a nearby K–12 independent girls' school. I accepted the position as I was eager to help with family finances and to stay close to science. Unexpectedly and quickly promoted to headmistress, I was surprised to discover that I enjoyed managing teaching and learning almost as much as I had managing experiments. Pleased that this meant I had developed some "life skills" while engaged in scientific investigations, I made my first "discovery" that scientific inquiry can help address life's problems as well as scientific ones! The faculty and I led Lenox successfully through the radical 1960s, using progressive educational philosophies and building attraction to and interest in science throughout the school. This job minimized work/family conflicts as my sons and I spent our days at adjacent schools, thus sharing school schedules, work interests and activities, and daily travel. I stayed in this position through all their school years. After they had left home for college, in 1972, I accepted a job as National Executive Director of Girl Scouts of the U.S.A. My responsibilities had escalated. I was now working with a large and distinguished board, and a few thousand employees, who, in turn, were responsible for millions of volunteers and Girl Scouts. Beyond managing this magnificent organization, I dealt with issues like relationships with Boy Scouts and other organizations, juvenile justice and girls' and women's rights. I was learning, for the first time, of the strength and value of the Girl Scouts leadership in informal, after-school teaching and learning in the sciences. Applying the spirit of the women's movement, I coined the phrase "Girl Scouting has been liberating American girls since 1913," which became a permanent feature on the cover of the Girl Scouts magazine. Tremendously proud of GSUSA and my work with it, I left, in 1975, to return home to deal with my family and a separation from my husband of twenty-six years.

CHAPTER SIX: Breaking a Corporate Ceiling

*The poet Keats said that science unweaves the rainbow.
I find the unweaving just as beautiful, beautiful in a
different way.*

—*Jonas Salk*

Thanks to the women's movement's bringing attention to the paucity of gender diversity in corporate leadership, my background in management and education attracted invitations to join corporate boards in the early 1970s. I accepted those from RCA and Avon Products (as its first female director) because I was familiar with some of the science of their products. This chapter includes stories of corporate men and women adjusting to a new world of power sharing, and relates how, at my young age with a lack of a business background, and relatively liberal politics, I was a minority in more than just gender. I was the only one on either board with any sci-tech experience, and noted many situations in which more sci-tech savvy among directors was badly needed and could have helped make more effective decisions. My directorship at RCA lasted until its merger with GE in 1985, and I served as an Avon director until 1999. Both experiences significantly enhanced my management and leadership knowledge and capabilities—while markedly strengthening my passion and arguments for science literacy for all. At a dinner celebrating my years with RCA, I suggested to other directors that it would help business and academe to better understand each other if they invited more academics to serve on boards with them.

CHAPTER SEVEN: Dr. Selby Goes to Washington

*To look for a black hat in a black room, you have to believe
it is there.*

— *Karl Popper, Philosopher*

In 1975, Endicott "Chub" Peabody, former governor of Massachusetts and retiring president of Americans for Energy Independence (AEI), a nonprofit organization based in Washington, DC, called to solicit my interest in succeeding him as president. Intrigued by the possibility of returning to nuclear energy, and of following my father's work in

Washington on science policy, I visited AEI's offices and was pleased that the organization's mission was to promote America's energy independence through conservation, coal and nuclear energy. Accepting the job, my arrival in Washington was greeted by the headline "Public Trust in Science is the Goal as the Lady Takes Over." To promote its mission, AEI needed the support of both scientists and the public. But as I soon discovered, in Washington, "educating the public" usually meant "lobbying" or "preaching" to influence opinion in a particular direction. Believing that teaching rather than "preaching" is the best way to increase trust between science and the public, I recommended that AEI's board reframe its mission around concepts such as marginal and replacement costs. These terms were already used and understood by the public, who must be engaged through familiar concepts and experience if they are to trust "expert" information. Soon deciding that I was an educator rather than a lobbyist, and that my future would not be in Washington, I resigned from AEI and returned to New York, and an amicable divorce from my husband.

CHAPTER EIGHT: None Can Keep Us from the Door

The quality of a nation is best known through the quality of its secondary schooling.
—*Nobel Laureate Wassily Leontief, Economist, 1979*

By 1979, weaknesses in high school science teaching were recognized as the "largest, most difficult single problem our country has" in statements by the chair of the National Academy of Sciences. In response, the State of North Carolina founded the North Carolina School of Science and Mathematics (NCSSM) in Durham, NC, the first tuition-free boarding school for gifted students in the U.S. Paul Ylvisaker, then Dean of Harvard's School of Education, suggested I learn more about the school, and introduced me to Wassily Leontief, Nobel Laureate in economics and board member of the sponsoring foundation, who invited me to join their efforts. Thus, after yet another fortuitous introduction, I was back in the world of science, never to leave it again. Beginning as a consultant, I conducted faculty searches and interviewed potential students and faculty, and then I was appointed the school's first dean. With my multiple perspectives, I helped design curriculum and helped to ensure that science was taught in its full societal, humanistic and artistic context. In 1980, we opened the school with 150 eleventh grade North Carolinian students: a racially integrated, economically diverse gathering of girls and boys. Helping design and operate this school provided an incomparable opportunity to draw from everything I had learned: in science, management, politics, teaching and learning. Every day brought gratification in watching students and teachers grow in the environment we created for them. Commuting back to Manhattan to see my family, I met my future husband, James Stacy Coles. In 1981, we married in New York with both our families, including the six children we now shared, all in attendance.

CHAPTER NINE: So Much More Friendly with Two

Only with a united effort of science and the humanities can we hope to succeed in discovering a community of thought, which can lead us out of the darkness, and the confusion, which oppress all mankind.
—NOBEL LAUREATE I.I. RABI, PHYSICIST, 1955

My new husband, well known as "Spike," was a physical chemist who had been engaged in World War II research for the Navy at the Woods Hole Oceanographic Institution (WHOI). Later, he became president of Bowdoin College and then president of Research Corporation, a nonprofit foundation for the advancement of science. Sharing roots in Woods Hole, we decided to spend our summers there and bought a house near both WHOI and the Marine Biological Laboratory (MBL). Soon after our marriage, I was appointed co-chair, with the distinguished Washington attorney William T. Coleman, of the first National Science Board commission to examine the status of U.S. precollege education in science, technology, engineering and mathematics. For our final report, in 1983, I wrote, "Science, formerly at the periphery of learning for a few, must now become center stage for all." This was the nation's first federal mandate for science education for all. Testimony we gathered from across the country prompted our recommendations for actions essential to introducing science education for all students: increased and enriched professional development of teachers, and expanded resources for informal education (including science and technology museums) and for technology education.

Now convinced that professional preparation and development of teachers is the weakest link in our education system, I accepted a position as professor of science education at New York University, eager to learn more about teacher education so I could most effectively promote it. There, I taught experienced New York City science teachers and graduate students. Working with a graduate student, Maura Flannery, I began to compare scientific inquiry with artistic inquiry, thereby developing a science/art context that remained, thereafter, central to my work. Paying new attention to technology, I collaborated with New York state education staff to place "industrial arts" within the academic curriculum, thereby closing the bothersome "brain versus brawn" dichotomy pervading most schools. A group of us were also asked by Commissioner of Education Tom Sobol to consider the desired student outcomes we believed should frame K–12 curriculum development. The nine outcomes we developed were approved and disseminated across the state. Political developments in Albany forced our report to move from establishing "desired student outcomes," which we defined as "what students should understand and be able to use," to "standards" for curriculum content. Soon, federal efforts to clarify educational curriculum adopted "standards" as their objective. Sadly, the focus on how students should be able to use their curriculum was lost, and parents and teachers are left now with curriculum "standards" rather than the much preferable "outcomes." After suffering with advanced Alzheimer's, my husband Spike's life came to an end in 1996, far too soon for me, but a welcome relief for him. Our families joined in Woods Hole to honor his life and loves. Our to-be-shared gravestone reads, "By their works shall ye know them."

CHAPTER TEN: Science Is a Personal and Democratic Inquiry

Science as something existing and complete is the most objective thing known to man. But science in the making, as an end to be pursued, is as subjective and psychologically conditioned as any other branch of human endeavor—so much so that the question "what is the purpose and meaning of science?" receives quite different answers at different times and from different sorts of people.

—ALBERT EINSTEIN, *1934*

"The girls and women of my country, as well as the boys and men, need knowledge of science and technology as much as they need reading and writing." These words, spoken by a Nigerian delegate at the 1995 United Nations Conference on Women I attended in Beijing, highlighted worldwide progress since our 1983 call for scientific literacy for all. Back in New York, in 1998 I designed and chaired a New York Academy of Sciences conference, "Choices and Successes: Women in Science and Engineering," that featured reports by senior male and female scientists covering workplace obstacles and remedies. Then, in 2000, Harvard's Radcliffe Institute invited me to initiate a Science, Society and Gender Center. This gave me precious time and resources to develop a platform for advancing women in science, and opening science for all. Arguments based on human rights, human capital and equal opportunity were then prevalent to help build supportive communities for women, but these arguments did not present evidence that engagement by women would benefit science. I found such evidence by illuminating that a scientist's personal perspectives influence what and how science is done. The scientist chooses and frames the question and chooses the observations and hypotheses with which to answer it. Thus, both science itself and the taxpayers supporting science deserve and need practitioners as diverse as the nation itself. Questions and searches for answers should be framed by diverse genders and diverse people. Exploring what makes science "science" also opens up arguments that make scientific processes more accessible to public use and understanding. Science is not governed by a singular Scientific Method. Instead it is a mode of inquiry initiated by human curiosity to ask and answer questions in ways similar to those practiced in the arts and humanities. Science asks questions of nature, but nature can only respond in the way the questions are asked; therefore, we learn more from nature when diverse people ask questions in diverse ways. Scientific inquiry deserves and needs equal opportunity with all other modes of inquiry to help advance human development. The book closes with the words of science teachers who believe that students should study and enjoy science because it is good for the world—and good for each one of us.

1

A New Spirit

Our work can seem like a pleasant hobby to us, it can sustain a sense of wonder, and bring us joy and fulfillment.
—HENRY STOMMEL, OCEANOGRAPHER

M Y MOTHER AND FATHER hoped I would be born on Valentine's Day, but I came a little early, arriving on February 4, 1927, at a maternity nursing home in Greenwich, a suburb southeast of London on the Thames River. Mother had chosen this place for my birth because it had been the home of J.M. Barrie, the author of Peter Pan, and she was impressed that the zero longitude line of Greenwich Mean Time went almost directly through the house. She liked the symbolism that her child's life would begin at longitudinal ground zero and be embraced by the spirit of Peter Pan! After Barrie's death, adherents of the religious philosophy and mysticism of theosophy bought his house and turned it into a nursing home. Her hopes for her child were certainly fulfilled by the special treatment she received after I was born. She woke up, not in the modest room she and my father had engaged, but in a spacious one, full of flowers and with a garden view. The theosophists told her the baby she had birthed was a "New Spirit" who deserved the best room in the house! Each time my mother told this story I thought how wonderful it would be if every child could be welcomed into the world with the hope and confidence of a New Spirit.

Although not theosophists, my mother and father certainly relished the thought that, after the devastation of World War I, they had brought something new and hopeful, a "New Spirit," into the world. They had met as classmates at the University of London just before

World War I. My mother, a classics student, was playing Cecily in a student performance of Oscar Wilde's *The Importance of Being Earnest*, and my father was the production's stage manager. His youth had been spent in a nearby country town where his father was the physician, while Mother was a born-and-bred Londoner. Her performance must have been notable because, at college, she became popularly known as "Cecily"—her character in the play.

Their college theater was, however, short-lived. At the start of World War I, my father, an honors student in chemistry and not quite eighteen, volunteered to join the army, and soon became an officer. He was sent to France, where, for four years, he fought in that war's ghastly trench warfare until hit by shrapnel shortly before the armistice of 1918. Framed and hanging on a wall in my home is a document, signed by Winston Churchill as Secretary of War, honoring Acting Captain Robert Keith Cannan for "gallant and distinguished services in the Field." There are other souvenirs of his years in the trenches that I treasure: books of poetry, small enough to be carried in his knapsack and now much tattered from such service. On their flyleaves he wrote: "Ypres 1917," "Le Cateau Oct 1918," and "Ypres Feb 1918," places famous for major World War I battles. In his knapsack, he carried little volumes of the poems of Keats, Matthew Arnold, John Ruskin, Swinburne, Rupert Brooke and Ralph Hodgson, poets famously treasured by his generation of British soldiers. He also left to me a larger folder of tattered leaves on which he had copied lines of poetry and witticisms and many references to my mother as "Cecily." Quotations from such works filled the years of our time together. When he lay dying, 54 years later, he described memories of bagpipers leading soldiers out of their trenches into hand-to-hand battle with the enemy. The last words I heard him say from his hospital bed were, "I can see the pipers coming over the hill."

Many more of my parents' male college friends perished in than survived the war, leaving, as my mother told me, a dearth of husbands for her female classmates. With a certain pride in her voice, she told me that she and her best friend were two of the few who found husbands after the war. When I asked her why I was an only child, born seven years after their post-war marriage, the only answer she would give was that my father had suffered from "shell shock" (today's post-traumatic stress disorder). No wonder she was ready for a New Spirit!

In 1930, we moved to New York City when my father, then a Senior Lecturer at University College, London, accepted the position of Professor of Chemistry at New York University's Medical College. England, still recovering from the war, was short on jobs for young scientists, so my father became part of Britain's post-war "brain drain." This move also returned him to the land of his birth. He had been born in California when his mother and his physician father moved there for a few years between medical studies in Edinburgh and postdoctoral work in London. By joining the British Army, he forfeited his dual citizenship. Thus, the three of us lived in New York as "resident aliens" until we became U.S. citizens after World War II.

"See that building over there? That is where we are going to live." These are the first words I remember hearing, while the distant view of an apartment building, decorated in mock Tudor style, is my first visual memory. I was three years old, sitting with my mother on top of a Fifth Avenue bus taking us from Manhattan to Queens. This was shortly after our arrival in New York so the view of a tall building in the distance visible over acres of shorter residential and office buildings was also my first long-distance view of the country to which I had come to live. This apartment house, in Jackson Heights, survives to this day, now surrounded by innumerable products of Queens' later building boom. Today, it is still visible from a subway window so I often look for it when taking the #7 elevated subway train for my frequent visits to the New York Hall of Science.

Other strong visual memories of those days reflect the Depression. I remember seeing and hearing a man singing in the garden enclosed by our apartment building, seeking contributions from its residents. I watched as my mother wrapped up coins in newspaper before throwing them to the singing man. When I asked her why she was doing this, she answered that the newspaper made it easier for him to find the coins in the grass and bushes below. Another strong memory of that apartment building is that my father painted one wall of my bedroom black. Why paint a wall black? So I could use it as a blackboard. I must have enjoyed and used it well, because it was on this blackboard that I designed a monogram for my name, using the three letters CEC embracing each other, and "ily" enclosed within that embrace.

Monogram design, 1931

In 1935, we moved from this apartment to an attached house nearby and I started school at Public School #69, an imposing dark brown brick building a few blocks away. I heard my parents say that in their wonderful new country they should be democratic and send me to one of its public schools rather than a private one. But my first day there did not start well. As we entered a classroom to meet my first teacher, I remember my mother telling the teacher that she thought Americans drank too much milk and that I should be excused from drinking it at "milk and cookie" morning break. I do remember my anger at Mother embarrassing me with words that started me in school as "different" from other students. How could she do that to me? I wanted to belong and be like everyone else. Sadly, I did move through school without feeling that I belonged to a class as she either agreed to or promoted my skipping a grade twice (done more frequently in those days), so that I ended up in the eighth grade at age 11. At this point she was tutoring me in math and Latin at home so I became really different in transferring to a boarding school in England for high school!

Try as I do, I can remember nothing of my elementary school beyond being pulled out of class with another boy to be told that we had high IQ test results. My reaction was mixed: annoyed once again to be recognized as different, but also proud that I had a good brain! Everything else about school must have washed over me like the Pledge of Allegiance we recited every morning: mishearing "for which it stands," I faithfully pledged allegiance to the flag "for Richard stands." When I was cleaning out some of my mother's old letters recently, I found a report card from PS 69. It recorded "S" for Satisfactory in all categories except for "Is generally careful" and penmanship. The same could be said about my penmanship and carefulness today. Some personal characteristics never do change!

My father commuted by subway to work at his office and chemistry laboratories at New York University's Medical College in Manhattan. Its main buildings were at First Avenue and 28th street, across the street from the large world-renowned Bellevue Hospital. Devoted to his research on protein chemistry, he often traveled to his labs on Sundays to check on his experiments, sometimes inviting me to come along as a special Sunday treat. It really was a treat to have quiet time alone with my father. One such Sunday, sitting next to him on the elevated subway traveling from Roosevelt Avenue in Queens to East 28th street in Manhattan, I noticed a man sitting across from us whose veins stood out visibly on his forehead. Asking my father what was wrong with him, he told me about the Depression, and explained that the enlarged veins showed he was ill, and probably sad because of being out of work. I kept worrying about this man when, later, I sat in my father's lab looking out the windows and watched patients and visitors streaming into the entrance of Bellevue Hospital, an immense dark building across the way. What troubles did they have? Why were they visiting the hospital? What was going to happen to them there? What could people in the hospital do to help them?

As unsettling as these questions were, I did love my visits to father's labs. I liked their smells, and their large airy rooms, empty when we visited, but full of lab benches, strange pipes weaving up and around the benches and funny-shaped glass everywhere. Each lab looked a little different, and some walls were covered with photos of doctors and students going back in time over several decades. They made me want to learn more about the interesting things men did there: things much more interesting, I decided, than what women I knew were doing with their time. Adding these early visits to years of experience that would come later, laboratories remain places where I always feel happy.

The things my mother and I did together were ballet classes, piano lessons and a few horseback riding lessons. Ballet lessons were given up early because my short legs could hardly reach the bar. However, it was thrilling to walk across the Metropolitan Opera stage (while no one was in the audience) on the way to class, and stand in front of the stage imagining what it would be like to perform in front of an audience. Learning about ballet positions did help me enjoy a lifetime of watching ballet, but piano lessons and daily practice were a continuing chore and obligation. Mother woke me up early every morning to practice for one hour before school, and then insisted I practice a second hour before supper. Thus, I was usually at the piano when my father got home from work to find me, seeking sympathy or admiration, plaintively playing a piece I thought he might enjoy. The piano "teaching" I received was just the kind I spent much of my later life fighting against: repetition upon repetition with no questions or thoughts of theory or composition that would have excited me. I have partially forgiven Mother for these enforced lessons because, later, she and I did share some good times at the piano, playing duets together and singing the English and European folk songs that she sang so well with her clear soprano voice. Indeed, her voice remains the kind of voice I most enjoy listening to and even tried to copy throughout the choral singing I enjoyed in years ahead. Later, during my school and college years, I loved accompanying family and friends singing and often worked out problems bothering me while playing Mozart's sonatas and Schubert's Impromptus. And I happily thank my mother for passing along to me her delight with English detective stories, perhaps my first introduction to "scientific" inquiries.

Learning that other children went to Sunday school, I asked if I could go too. My parents had grown up with different familial Protestant affiliations and no commitment to one or the other, so they decided to look for something different and chose a local Christian Science church because "some very nice people belong there." For this choice I am forever grateful. In my mind's eye, I can still see the words "God Is Love" inscribed in large letters above the church's unadorned altar. In its Sunday school I learned that human beings are born imperfect, not sinful. Only God is perfect, so the best we can do is try to come as close to God's perfection as we can. I have long felt blessed by this approach to faith and morality, finding the burden of imperfection much easier—and more productive—to live with than the burden of sin. I had little trouble disregarding other Christian Science teachings about medicine. My father was a medical scientist, so I simply shut my ears quickly and easily, as perhaps only a ten-year-old can, to anything negative about doctors or medicine.

Loneliness—a feeling that something really fun and interesting was missing—and an active imagination and unshakeable curiosity marked my childhood. As an only child, with no relatives on my side of the Atlantic, I was frequently alone, and encouraged to be independent, For example, when traveling with my parents I was urged to explore the station by myself and find my way back to where they were. And yet, sometimes, rather than being encouraged to ask questions, I recall Mother calling me "Little Miss Know-It-All." Was this because I was asking too many questions? Or was she telling me that it is not good for a girl to be curious and knowledgeable? It was probably the latter because in my teenage years she told me not to argue because "men don't like it."

Without siblings or relatives in the U.S., there was nothing to do at home in Queens but read and practice the piano. I do not recall "play dates" that later became a great part of my children's, and their children's, lives. Instead, I fantasized about many things, including three particular wishes that I developed in my pre-adolescent years: for an older brother, horn-rimmed glasses and a library. Later, the older brother morphed into boyfriends and husbands, horn-rimmed glasses into knowledge and the library into academic institutions!

Our modest lives were enlivened by visits every third summer to England and excursions from there to Austria and Switzerland. How wonderful those trips were! I was never seasick crossing the Atlantic and was allowed to eat almost anything I wanted from the plentiful menus, to slide down long banisters, and to run around the decks. And visiting my English aunts and uncles and two sets of grandparents was a treat. With them, I was allowed to eat the sweet desserts and bread-and-butter sandwiches that were restricted treats at home. We played card and board games and went for walks in parks and woods, again something we didn't do in New York. Occasionally meeting my four first cousins, all boys, was a special experience, although later we mourned for one lost at Dunkirk, where so many other British soldiers lost their lives in World War II.

First rowing lesson with father, Woods Hole Harbor, 1933

In years that did not feature trips across the Atlantic, we spent summers in Woods Hole. My father moved his research projects and medical students from his laboratories in New York to this place for biologists' work, and science, and play on Cape Cod, Massachusetts. It became my "hometown," my place of lasting memories of families and friends, the place I still keep coming back to. Beaches and bays, rocks and islands encircle its small village and large laboratories. The masts of sailboats, some very tall, some less so, poke into every view. Here science could mean studying jellyfish, their translucent flesh reflecting the sunset outside laboratory windows; exploring invertebrates on the beaches and marshes nearby; or reading in the Marine Biological Laboratory library where Rachel Carson, Albert Szent-Gyorgi, Jonas Salk and Gertrude Stein also read and wrote. And all is set in the "shining sea" invoked in "America the Beautiful" by Katherine Lee Bates, who was born and lived in nearby Falmouth. Most of the summer months of my youth were spent in this lovely, lively place. I learned from a story a neighbor's son wrote of his childhood that his parents paid $2,200 in 1930 to purchase their home just a door away from us, so my parents must have paid a similar amount for our little cottage. All of the homes along Gardiner Road were just a few feet from a pond, a short walk from the beach, and close to the "Mess" where, in the early years, we all could take our meals. The long history of science in Woods Hole began with establishment of a temporary fisheries laboratory in 1871 that today has expression as the Northeast Fisheries Laboratory of the National Oceanic and Atmospheric Administration. Next came the Marine Biological Laboratory (MBL), founded in Woods in 1888 as an outgrowth of the efforts of Boston women science teachers seeking to provide opportunities for science teachers and students to engage in "the practical study of marine forms." The nearby Woods Hole Oceanographic Institution, founded in 1930, was small in my youth but today is a world leader in ocean sciences. The Woods Hole Research Center and a laboratory of the U.S. Geological Survey are also based in Woods Hole, and the National Academy of Sciences has a site atop the lovely Quissett Harbor for summer conferences and study groups. *The New Yorker* published a cartoon some years ago with the caption "The leisure of the theory classes." For me, this perfectly describes Woods Hole as a place that provides leisure, and much more, for members of biology's theory class!

Gertrude Stein was an early visitor to the Marine Biological Laboratory. Local postcards show her in boots and long skirt, with a group digging on the seashore. Rachel Carson repeatedly credited her knowledge about and devotion to the ocean to the several summers she studied there. Following her college years, in 1929 she spent six weeks at the MBL as a beginning investigator in zoology and returned in 1932 for embryological research. In 1949, Carson took a ten-day trip on a fisheries vessel named *Albatross*, traveling from Woods Hole to Georges Bank, during which she wrote parts of her second book, *The Sea Around Us*. Carson returned again in 1951 to spend July and August in Woods Hole. To honor her memory, there is now a beautiful life-size sculpture of her sitting on the harbor waterfront with a book on her lap, regarding the ocean beyond. I like to imagine her sitting there forever.

A statue of Rachel Carson overlooks Woods Hole Harbor at the Marine Biological Laboratory in Woods Hole, MA. (Photo by Tom Kleindinst)

During these years, my father selected several students from his first-year medical school chemistry class to work in his MBL laboratory over the summer. Jonas Salk, one of those selected, worked on the reaction between formaldehyde and proteins during his summer in the lab. Later, this is the reaction he used to create his world-changing polio vaccine. My father was Jonas's first mentor, and introduced his first published research paper. I well remember thinking how very nice he was to me when he visited our house. During the close friendship we later developed, Jonas spoke with me about his beginnings as a poor boy from the Bronx who chose medicine, at first, as a way to "get out of the ghetto," until my father brought him to Woods Hole. There, he said, "I discovered research, and there was no turning back." Referring to Woods Hole in a letter to my father's widow, he wrote, "In a way it all began there." Jonas also liked to remind me that I had snubbed his bride when he brought her to meet our family. Apparently this notable medical scientist also brought me my first experience with jealousy!

Virtually none of us children of summer scientists went away to camp; a full outdoor and social life was available to us in this community where at least one of our parents worked. We sailed and swam, played tennis and square-danced, getting where we needed to by bicycle or on foot. During the gas rationing of World War II, my assignment was to bicycle to buy meat for the family at the nearest butcher, four miles away in Falmouth. We found our summer reading in the village's stone-walled library, and a local church bell rang daily at noon and 6 PM to remind us of lunch and dinner times. In the early 1940s, I bicycled barefoot around the village wearing blue jeans and a boy's shirt with its tails hanging out. Dealing later with my own sons' adolescence, I decided that no culture shock their generation gave me could match the contrast between the Victorian London of my parents' youth and that of their barefoot tomboy daughter by the seaside. There were no barriers, familial or cultural, to my choosing to be a "tomboy," to do what the boys were doing. Taught to sail by a neighbor's son, I crewed for him in his eighteen-foot knockabout during weekly races. When I could hoist the spinnaker faster than anyone else in the fleet, he was as proud of me as he would have been of a younger brother. After races, girls participated in all the "dirty work," scrubbing the hulls, folding the sails and hauling up the dinghies. At home, too, with no son to call upon, my father expected me to clean and oil my bicycle and help him with heavy garden chores. There was no brother or sister with whom I had to compete for my father's attention. While swimming with my father, he taught me to stand on his shoulders to dive into the water (what could be a greater thrill for a young girl who loved and trusted her father!) and to hit and return a tennis ball. Now, when science teachers encourage girls to get messy doing hands-on laboratory and field work, I appreciate how profoundly my Woods Hole youth prepared me to feel comfortable rolling up my sleeves. When I was sixteen, Woods Hole also brought me my first boyfriend. Sitting beneath a lighthouse, watching the lively sea below, Eddy and I talked about the science we might do in our futures and experimented with a first kiss. As a future scientist, he exhibited good scientific curiosity when he asked, "Do you know where the noses go?"

During my childhood, "science" meant the smell of formaldehyde in my father's lab or sunrise boat rides around neighboring islands collecting squid that the Marine Biological Laboratory then sent to laboratories throughout the world. I knew scientists as nice friendly people: young and old, male and female, diverse in the languages they spoke and in their personalities, tastes and styles. Local lore says that "more Nobel Laureates pass through the doors of the Marine Biological Laboratory than anywhere but Stockholm." They walked past our cottage on their way to the post office and the beach. Professors played their recorders in one another's homes and talked with eager sun-tanned students. Priests, nuns and all manner of visitors from all corners of the earth took courses or worked in our laboratories. When laboratory lights remained lit at night, we knew scientists were babysitting their experiments. And a few of them were women. One in particular was the mother of a girlfriend, so I knew of women who were scientists, even parents, and Father spoke of them as respected colleagues.

Surrounded all summer by scientists, I started to relate each one's preferences and personalities to the kinds of work they chose to do, and how they chose to do it. Some loved going outdoors on field trips, asking questions and seeking answers about the shapes, structures and behaviors of plants or animals. Some stayed in libraries (nowadays they would be on computers), asking questions about what other scientists have done. Others worked in their laboratories, asking questions about the compositions and interactions of chemicals. Reading Hendrik Willem van Loon's popular *The Story of Mankind* sticks in my memory, undoubtedly because its stories reinforced what I was learning about how different people, following their different talents and interests, choose different ways, different modes of inquiry, through which to express themselves . . . whether in painting, writing, building, math or science.

As I was learning about science and scientists in Woods Hole, I was also learning about teaching and learning through attending very diverse schools. My parents' closeness to family and friends in England prompted them to send me back there to boarding school at age eleven when English parents often chose to dispatch their sons and daughters to schools away from home. In September 1938, during the days now known as "Munich Week," we were in London readying me for my English school. We stood along Piccadilly watching the parade to celebrate Prime Minister Neville Chamberlain's return from his infamous meeting with Hitler, rejoicing in the "peace in our time" we all thought he had negotiated. I was wearing my brand-new school uniform for the first time. Happy and proud that my school's distinctive ribbon in the hatband of my beautiful Panama straw and the school crest on the pocket of my blazer told the world that I belonged to the tribe of Wycombe Abbey School.

This was also the time in which we heard, by cable, that our Woods Hole house had been virtually destroyed by the 1938 hurricane. During the storm, a tidal wave surged over the nearby beach, then down the adjacent road and swept our little house away. After crossing the pond it came to rest on the town's baseball field. A cable from the Falmouth Town Council informed my father that the baseball season could not begin unless and until our house was removed from the park! So Father sent instructions to remove it while some year-round neighbors spent part of their following winter cleaning mud from the filigree design in some of my parents' china! Later that winter, after retuning to the U.S., my parents wrote that they thought it best to sell our now empty property rather than rebuild. Apparently I complained mightily that this option would leave me with no place to call home. They then reversed course and hired a builder to construct another house according to the design my father sketched on graph paper.

At Wycombe Abbey, I was considered American, and the only one among the 250 girls in the school. The Abbey occupied 250 acres surrounding a small hill in High Wycombe, a town halfway between London and Oxford. The handsome main Gothic buildings were surrounded by beautifully kept grounds containing 25 tennis courts, 25 cricket pitches and lacrosse fields, a swimming pool, a small lake and even a classic maze of privet hedge at the top of the hill. Rather than resenting Wycombe Abbey's highly disciplined culture, I was happy there. It was something to belong to and more fun than being at home. The girls and teachers were nice to me even though I was a "foreigner." I did hear that the word went around that the American didn't know how to butter her bread. In England, butter is spread on the end of a loaf of unsliced bread before it is sliced, not afterwards, as I was used to. I was trying hard to belong, so I changed to this useful way of thin-slicing bread!

As a new girl in Butler House, one of the residential houses on the school campus, an older girl, a "prefect," took me aside to tell me about House rules and customs. She asked if I knew what the word "bumptious" meant. I did not, but I was not going to admit my ignorance to her, so I answered "yes," whereupon she told me that the most important thing to remember, as a young newcomer, was not to be "bumptious." She illustrated this point by telling me I was not allowed to sit around the fire in the living room unless and until I was invited. Since there was no central heating, only fireplaces, this sounds horrible, but in practice it wasn't because the entire mood was friendly and I was usually noticed and invited in; no need to be bumptious in order to stay warm!

After the U.S. entered World War II, the school buildings and grounds became the headquarters of the American Eighth Air Force. When I visited the school after the war, I was profoundly moved to read these words, engraved on a large plaque in the school's main entrance above Winston Churchill's signature: "In these buildings were conceived and directed the plans which led to the destruction of the Nazi Air Force."

Years later, meeting a couple of airmen who had been stationed at our school during the war, I laughed to hear them tell of the sign over the buzzer next to each dormitory bed that read: "If in distress in the middle of the night, call the Mistress." Our teachers were mistresses, not masters, but in all other respects Wycombe Abbey could have been a boys' school. Our uniform included ties to wear with our shirts. Before breakfast, which meant before sunrise in the winter, senior girls would take us outside to practice catching cricket balls. Catching solid wooden balls on a cold morning hurt one's bare hands, but I loved the camaraderie.

In classes I dutifully accepted my father's instruction to work hard and do well. In math, I learned to add, multiply and subtract in pounds, shillings and pence—a new and different task for me as British money was not yet on a decimal system and all accounting had to be done in base 12 rather than 10. In remedial penmanship, I was happy with my assigned task to copy from articles in *National Geographic* since it allowed me to read the magazine. Science classes were about trees and leaves and how they were fed. After we were told that capillary action enabled water to climb up a tree through its roots and leaves, I asked the first question I recall that could have been called a scientific one, "How can water climb up if the force of gravity is pulling it down?" Not satisfied by the answer I was given, this question stayed with me, unanswered for some years. Sadly, memories of learning about the shapes and names of leaves and trees lasted no time at all . . . although now I dearly wish they had! Wycombe Abbey honored girls' achievements, whether in sports, music or academics. This is where my ambition to attend Oxford or Cambridge started, as many of the school's graduates attended one of those institutions and were honored for doing so. I recently unearthed a copy of the school's alumnae magazine, in which I noticed that university honors earned by its graduates were given attention equivalent to that of personal ones in alumni news. But a British university was not to be in my future.

In July of 1939, I returned home to New York City, traveling alone aboard the last pre-war civilian trip of the great Cunard liner *Aquitania*. Traveling alone, I was free to eat whatever I liked and so cherish a photo of me at the table with five or six other women, all probably teachers on vacation, with my plate very full of food—theirs only sparsely filled. I particularly remember treating myself by ordering heavy cream (not milk as at home!) on my morning Grape-Nuts. This good eating, coupled with finding the pleasantest reading spot on the deck, made my summer school assignment of a classic nineteenth century novel about the Black Death a little easier. At Wycombe, we had conducted practice drills for entering air raid shelters and been given gas masks. Proud of this symbol of my English life, I wore it around my neck on arrival at the dock in New York in July 1939. With war so imminent, I had to forgo any thoughts of another year's schooling in England.

My next school was radically different. Fortunately for me, my mother chose The Dalton School, a New York institution, then a leader in the progressive movement in education. This school promoted and practiced some very different ideas about teaching and learning. For two weeks in the ninth grade we cared for and studied babies who spent their days in our school nursery, and we city girls were delighted with the novelty of visiting a farm and milking cows. We were also introduced to sculpture, where I learned to form clay into figures I still admire in my home today. We discussed issues of the day in social studies, rather than the history of kings and queens. I was surprised and honored when the biology teacher brought me a cow's heart from a butcher shop, and I explored its valves and muscles with my fingers as he suggested. His gift of this bloody tissue told me he identified me as someone who could enjoy science.

At his suggestion, I learned the names of all the bones of the body and can remember them to this day.

Sculpting clay at The Dalton School, 1940

My one year at Dalton brought learning of all kinds. Then a school for girls only, Dalton was a "progressive" school where students' original questions and opinions were, and still are, honored. We were encouraged to think for ourselves. In social studies, I suggested, in a homework essay, that all humans could enjoy immortality through how they are remembered after their deaths . . . by those still alive. I was astonished to have this essay of mine discussed in class. An idea of mine valued by others, and immortal itself, at least in the sense that it has lived on in my own memory since I was twelve years old! Some education that year also occurred off campus. I learned to change my path when I believed a strange man was following me as I walked home from the subway to my apartment building after school. And one afternoon a friend and I played hooky and sat in the last row of the Paramount Theater on Broadway to hear Frank Sinatra sing "Ol' Man River."

After another summer in Woods Hole, I returned to boarding school at my own request. Happy as I was at the Dalton School, I missed outdoor life, athletics and the company of friends, night and day. Life at home was very quiet. This time I went to a school in Toronto called Havergal Ladies College, where I completed the fifth year of high school in the British system. Even though I was not prepared for Havergal's traditional English curriculum and I was still two years younger than my classmates, I managed with the confidence that Dalton had given me to tackle any subject. I was much more comfortable talking freely in class and with teachers than were students who had never been in informal, progressive classrooms. In fairness, I do remember joking that at the Dalton School one could "talk and talk and say nothing." While Havergal's teachers did not actively solicit student ideas or opinion, they did not turn them down when offered. When I presented the math teacher with an alternative proof of the Pythagorean Theorem, she said it was "interesting": she did not reject it. And I wasn't the only student to raise an uncommon question in class—I remember admiring the student who asked why the Wife of Bath wore red stockings! Apparently I not only loved asking questions, but also admired those who did!

In those days, students were commonly tracked into either academic or nonacademic courses of study. Assigned to the academic track at Havergal, courses in shop, studio art, cooking or health were not open to me, while math and science were not open to students in the nonacademic track. At our fiftieth reunion, a classmate told me of her lifelong struggle to recover the sense of self-worth she lost when assigned to the nonacademic track in "domestic science." This assignment implied that her mind was not as valuable or potentially useful as other minds—her brothers,' or mine. Later, she enjoyed a full life, catching up on scholarly ideas and reading, albeit always deprecating her own intellectual skills. And for my part, my scientific laboratory work could have been improved had I also had the option to engage in the practical skills of studio art and shop. And life would have been richer had I not maintained the belief that I couldn't paint or draw or build things.

Canada had joined Britain in World War II, so most of my classmates had fathers and/or brothers fighting overseas. A dear friend lost her brother shortly after he had charmed me by showing off his Army kilt with its fourfold pleats of Scottish wool. In morning assemblies we sang "There'll Always Be an England" and prayed for "those in peril on the sea." I watched soldiers parade the streets of Toronto before embarking for their fate at the infamously almost suicidal landing of Allied troops at the French port of Dieppe, just as during Cape Cod summers I watched from our porch when convoys gathered in Buzzards Bay and disappeared overnight to cross the Atlantic. We knew that some ships and soldiers would make it safely back, and many others would not.

Students sent by their parents from England to Canada for their safety were called "evacuees" and became some of my best friends. My roommate, Carol, and I daily recorded on our wall map the sites of aerial battles and the numbers of planes and casualties reported in the newspaper. I visit Carol whenever I am in England, and we often recall these school days together—including our daring climb out of our bedroom window one night and onto an adjacent roof. Living with many different girls certainly helped me enjoy the friendship of many and different women throughout my life. So often I relate a new woman friend to someone I knew well in boarding school. One tall beautiful blonde from Nova Scotia made an impression on New York's Fifth Avenue when she insisted on carrying her skis on her shoulder on her way to my apartment from the train. Another married a soldier during her senior year, telling us tales that brought some needed sex education to us virginal students.

Our home library included books by scientists and mathematicians of the day: Max Born, Bertrand Russell, Lancelot Hogben, James Jeans and Albert Einstein. They described, in eloquent prose, science's way of knowing. Nineteenth-century novels, together with my mother's favorite detective stories, taught me most of the psychology, sociology and history I learned in these early years. My only formal sex education came in a book I found conspicuously lying on the coffee table. I was told, pointedly, that it would be interesting for me to read. As I recall, it included something about eggs and fertilization—not anything about what humans do!

Despite my friendly Woods Hole and family introduction to science, my love affair with it did not begin until a Havergal chemistry teacher introduced the periodic table of the elements. My memory readily recalls the classroom and where I was sitting when the teacher told us about the particular numerical and structural relationships it reveals between all the elements on our planet. Over a hundred years ago, the Russian scientist Dmitri Mendeleev observed that when he arranged the known elements (e.g., carbon, hydrogen, uranium) in order of their increasing atomic weight, there was a behavioral similarity between every eighth element in the series. If the series is divided into groups of eight and these groups are placed under each other in successive rows, the elements in each vertical column correspond to each other in chemical properties. Later investigations revealed that the number and placement of electrons orbiting around the nucleus of each element's atom explain the shared behavior among the groups of eight. That numbers could have a role in governing atomic behavior was the most astonishing idea that had yet crossed my path. Magical, it seemed to me, that physical behavior and numbers could relate to each other in nature.

A book given to me as Havergal's science prize, *The Restless Universe*, helped me understand this magic. The British physicist and Nobel Laureate Max Born opened his 1936 book with these words:

> *It is odd to think that there is a word for something which, strictly speaking, does not exist, namely, "rest." We distinguish between living and dead matter; between moving bodies and bodies at rest. This is a primitive point of view. What seems dead, a stone or the proverbial "door-nail," say, is actually forever in motion.*

I read these words again and again, finding magic and poetry in them, and exploring the significance of his "odd" thought about a universe made of tiny always-moving particles, invisible to the eye. In the margins of each page of this book were sequential drawings of the movement of such particles. They presented an animated cartoon when the pages were flipped rapidly. This blend of ideas and images showed me that mathematics and science do work together to relate form and function. Traveling in Russia in the 1960s, I was delighted to see some of the "beauty" I was discovering in science displayed in public places for all to see. Busts of famous Russian scientists were installed on subway platforms, and in St. Petersburg, I saw a mural of the periodic table covering an entire outside wall of the house where Mendeleev had lived.

The magic that stirred my youth did not just come from science. Lines written by Yeats, Shelley, Keats, Milton and Byron dominated the English classes I remember and that still resonate in my memory. The artistic and sensual magic my adolescence found in nineteenth century romantic British poetry has stayed with me for a lifetime. These lines from Tennyson's "Lochsley Hall" stunned me with their technological predictions as much as their poetry:

> *Saw the heavens fill with commerce, argosies of magic sails,*
> *Pilots of the purple twilight, dropping down their costly bales:*
> *Heard the heavens fill with shouting, and there rained a ghastly dew*
> *From the nations' airy navies grappling in the central blue.*

That the artistic capacity of a poet could imagine a future that science and technology had not yet dreamed of awoke me to power in the arts. Perhaps it is this revelation that led me to dwell for years on the following lines from Yeats:

> *Could man be drunk forever, with liquor, love, or fights,*
> *Lief should I rouse at morning and lief lie down of nights.*
> *But men at whiles are sober, and think by fits and starts,*
> *And when they think they fasten a hand upon their hearts.*

Somehow, I knew, even then, that hearts do have their place in sober science: a nice thought from a New Spirit!

2

A Female Harvard in Wartime

The art of research is that of making a problem solvable by finding out ways of getting at it.
—Peter Medawar, Biologist, 1979

IN THE SPRING OF 1943, my father and I embarked on that annual ritual of educational buying and selling: the parent/child college tour. Radcliffe College was our last stop. We had admired Wellesley's expansive green grounds and Gothic buildings, but I had long enjoyed landscaped lawns, trees, and gray stone buildings in boarding school. I now hankered to start doing what the boys were doing—in coed classes and at a cosmopolitan university. I still dreamed of Oxford and Cambridge, but their country was at war, fighting for its life. Without England as an option, I was ready to return to the United States, and dropped the University of Toronto from consideration. Neither Princeton nor Yale yet admitted women, so Radcliffe's access to Harvard and Boston made it my obvious first choice.

While passing through Harvard Yard on the way to Radcliffe's offices, the words "Enter to Grow in Wisdom" inscribed over one of Harvard's gates resonated romantically with my dreams, reinforcing delight with all I saw. After exploring the hubbub of Harvard Square, we walked a few blocks up busy Brattle and bucolic Garden Streets to the quiet green Radcliffe quadrangle. At the Admissions Office I was pleased to learn that the graduate school dean, Bernice Brown Cronkhite, would interview me. My father and I sat comfortably in her office, admiring the flowering apple trees framing the view out the windows, when she walked in and introduced herself. Well-known for her leadership at Radcliffe, Dean Cronkhite was gracious, welcoming and treated me as an adult. Learning from my school record that I had led my class academically and had passed Canadian Senior matriculation examinations, then equivalent to completing a 13th year of American high school, she recommended that I skip the freshman year and enter Radcliffe as a sophomore. Having no idea whether beginning college as a sixteen-year old sophomore was a good or bad idea, my response was governed by wartime, and knowing that studying was all I could do to help, I accepted being placed, once more, ahead of my age group. Only now, looking back, do I recall my insecurities in starting a new educational venture, once again as "different." As the youngest in my class and a British citizen from a Canadian school, I certainly was an "outsider." Mother would have preferred Wellesley, and later said that I "lost my good manners" in Cambridge, but my choice of Radcliffe was faithful to the three childhood wishes I still remembered: for an older brother, horn-rimmed glasses and a library. Radcliffe/Harvard could surely provide the learning and seeing tools I needed. Eddy, my first boyfriend, was already at Harvard, and although not an older brother, there were certainly other boys to be found on campus, and, I assumed, horn-rimmed glasses could come with age. Finally, the university was effectively a library of everything, so it appeared my wishes would become reality.

I arrived in Cambridge in the fall of 1943 dressed in a tailored suit and laced-up shoes, not a "Sloppy Joe" sweater and loafers like everyone else. Mother thought suits were what educated young ladies should wear and that loafers were bad for your feet, and I had given up arguing with her. Despite my fears in being an "outsider," thanks to friendly classmates and professors, I soon felt comfortable. Even with World War II as a constant backdrop, my three years at Radcliffe/Harvard were decidedly happy ones.

To enable potential servicemen to graduate in three years, Harvard had initiated an accelerated wartime program of three semesters per year. Radcliffe, then an independent college with its own board of trustees, joined in. A year after I arrived, in the fall of 1944, Harvard's Faculty of Arts and Sciences was given "complete responsibility for the program of instruction of students in Radcliffe College at both the undergraduate and graduate levels." For us Radcliffe students there was no obvious difference since we already had access to Harvard courses and professors. During my years there, Radcliffe students lived separately from Harvard students, in Radcliffe's own dormitories surrounding a landscaped grass rectangle known as the Quad. It was a pleasant walk from there, past local residences and churches echoing Cambridge's colonial history, to the small collection of handsome red-brick classroom and office buildings where Radcliffe-only classes were held. The main quadrangle in the midst of these classroom buildings was Radcliffe Yard, where some introductory classes for Radcliffe students only were held. Five minutes from Harvard Yard, it was much smaller, less crowded and had more gardens and greenery.

Military uniforms were everywhere in Cambridge, just as they had been in Toronto. Most of the uniforms belonged to ROTC and Navy V-12 students taking short-term courses, and to Army draftees in the Army Specialized Training Program (ASTP). The only male members of my class of 1946 were those disqualified for military service. Military contracts providing instruction and room for officers in training enabled Harvard to fill its residential houses and to keep professors employed while regular students were away on military duty. My science and math classes were filled with students assigned there by the Army or Navy. Uniformed women, female Naval Ensigns known as WAVES (Women Accepted for Voluntary Emergency Service) attended Harvard classes. They were billeted in a Radcliffe dormitory, emptied out to accommodate them. This left Radcliffe short of residential rooms, so the college found alternate housing for transfer students like me. Thus, as a sophomore transfer student, I first lived in an off-campus house where a gentle housemother and a small band of other transfer students provided an easy, friendly introduction to college life. It was reassuring to come "home" after class to a residential house with a few house-mates. My next move was to a small Radcliffe dormitory, leaving it soon thereafter, again to provide space for the WAVES. When I moved to the larger Briggs Hall, my room was just above the entranceway: a great place for viewing dates sharing a goodnight kiss!

Both Radcliffe and Harvard did their best to retain some pre-war campus life, including college dances: Radcliffe's were called "Jolly Ups." Accompanying Eddy to a dance at his residence hall, Lowell House, I was probably the only one there who was enjoying her very first dressed-up dance. At sixteen years old with Eddy as my "date," when the band played "Good Night, Sweetheart," I recall absolute delight with my surroundings. That song became so familiar as it closed virtually every dance in those days. The Copley Plaza Hotel in Boston offered "Waltzing Parties." If we found dates to escort us and had long evening dresses to wear, we could indeed waltz all evening, wearing the flower corsages boys provided. In my copy of the *Oxford Book of English Verse*, I saved the petals of each corsage I received over those years, and listed the initials of the boys who gave them to me. This collection of English poetry with its list of initials and dried petals has remained on a shelf in my home ever since.

Singing was a welcome pastime during the war. Soon after arriving on campus, I joined the Harvard/Radcliffe Glee Club, whose annual highlight was singing Bach's B Minor in Boston's Symphony Hall. Conductor Serge Koussevitzky's worldwide fame contrasted with the rough language he used in rehearsal while criticizing his equally famous organist, E. Power Biggs. Joining dozens of other choristers, behind the orchestra, facing the audience in that grand hall was my first experience performing on a significant stage. The Harvard Glee Club did a great job in maintaining its rehearsals, concerts and traditional spirit during wartime years, fostering my participation in small choral groups for years to come.

Through my grandchildren, I have learned about the differences between college life today and that of ours decades ago. Campus features like glee clubs and debate teams remain similar, while differences now involve daily habits such as eating and cleaning clothes. We had no washing machines to use, so many of us mailed dirty laundry home in boxes to be returned to us from home, washed and ironed and in the same boxes. During my first year, Harvard eliminated its waitress service at meals and offered students these jobs instead. Never having taken a waitress job during the summer, as many friends had, I was curious about the work and thought it would be interesting to hear conversations at more than one table . . . and earn some pocket money too. After I volunteered to do so, I was surprised that my parents argued against it. I wondered if their negative reaction reflected the greater class bias and academic focus of the British universities they knew, but I never asked.

While Eddy and his friends made my social entry to Harvard easy, academic choices were difficult. I had no idea what I wanted to study. Starting college as a sophomore, I had to choose a department immediately, and the department would assign me a tutor. Not yet committed to any single subject and not yet knowing Harvard courses, I first chose mathematics, as so many students do who are told they are "good at math." I was good at reading and writing too, but somehow being "good at math" carries with it an obligation to do something for the world that others think they cannot do. If my studies were going to help the world, I figured they had to be useful, and mathematics was recognizably useful. I walked into my tutor's office to see him leaning back in his chair with his saddle shoes on his desk. He was Garrett Birkhoff, the son of the very famous mathematician of the same name. He took one look at the sixteen-year-old girl standing in front of him and said, "Let's study the lives of famous mathematicians." This response made me so angry that my mathematics major lasted only a semester. I wanted to study math, not history! I felt I was being denigrated as a young female. When I sat down, he gave me a copy of a big fat book called *Lives of Famous Mathematicians* and suggested I select a mathematician to study. I have no memory of whom I selected, but I do remember feeling better when he gave me a key to the private mathematics library in Harvard's eminent Widener Library. Searching out this private library in the back hall of Widener made me feel closer to mathematics than had my professor's history assignment. Soon, I felt more recognized when Professor Birkhoff later gave me a description of the work I could complete as an undergraduate thesis: "a rigorous and thorough proof of the Laplace transformation using only real numbers." He told me it would be included in a book he was writing. However, I was already deciding that math was lonely and Laplace transformations—about which I now remember nothing—were too far from the "real world," so I started considering other courses. My father's subject of chemistry was never an option for me. When I dropped a dish, he would remark, "You'll never be a chemist." Despite Woods Hole's influence, I had no interest in biology. I thought it was about categorizing different plants and species and memorizing their long Latin names. Urged by Eddy and his roommate, Alex, and a book on the philosophy of physics that I had been reading, I turned to physics.

To discuss this switch in my major, I met with Professor Otto Oldenberg, a stately and gracious gentleman, then head of the Physics Department. He greeted me cordially, explained that a concentration in physics did not include a tutor or senior thesis and showed me around the physics classrooms in the Jefferson Laboratories building. Much as I grew to love the people and what transpired in that building—it does look ugly from the outside—formidable physics was happening inside. The only warming feature was the broad steps that led to the entrance, which were handy for chatting and reading notes quickly before class. Further encouraged by Eddy and his friends, I made the switch to physics. Apparently it was not a smooth transition because, in a letter to a "round robin" of boarding school friends, I wrote:

> . . . *in all subjects I've found my preparation wasn't enough—however I've survived, but I hate to find out how much Chem I don't know. I have math and physics at Harvard and girls are definitely in the minority—what a difference to have male competition in these courses— Yipe!—I certainly like it better—and no remarks! I must admit that there are other interests in physics since Ken sits next to me!*

As difficult as my shift to physics may have been, it certainly went better than my first chemistry lab. Assigned to determine the boiling point of sulfuric acid, my classmates and I took positions along both sides of a laboratory bench where we were each assigned a Bunsen burner, a thermometer, and a flask in which to heat the acid. Not sufficiently careful with the flask, some boiling acid sputtered up near my face. A neighboring student saw this happen and rushed me to an overhead sprinkler to shower away any touch of acid. Forever grateful to this young man whose quick thinking saved me from any damage, I remain particularly appreciative of "first responders" in any emergency.

After I became a registered physics student, many of the physics students were invited to see a new wartime electronic invention. Called an oscilloscope, it was distinguished by a fluorescent screen on which we could see images of simple sinusoidal waves moving from left to right. We were told they were images of an electric current passing through the equipment. Until then, we could only imagine electrical waves through mathematical descriptions: drawings and graphs simulating their mathematics. This new technology, then called a cathode ray tube, directly exhibited a pattern made by electrical waves on a fluorescent screen, the screen we know today as our TV screen. None of us that day could have imagined the world of imaging on TV, phone and computer screens that was to come. But, immediately, I was bothered, not thrilled by this engineering innovation. Perfectly satisfied with my own mental mathematical model of electrical waves, at first I resented the technologically manufactured image. It intruded on my imagination. I mention this only because it illuminates that as long as I can remember, I have been more interested in ideas and theories than in facts and practical applications. As a student, I found Maxwell's four equations describing electricity and magnetism much more interesting than the electrical and magnetic phenomena themselves. Mechanics was almost boring for me, while the theory of light and the nature and behavior of waves, energy, atoms and their sub-particles were not. Years later, my second husband, a physical chemist, could not understand how I, a former physics student, did not know how a radio worked, or why my attraction to all kinds of oddities did not extend to technological ones. Was this personal reaction prompted by the absence of any practical "hands-on" mechanical experiences in my female-gendered youth? Was it because I did not read *Popular Mechanics* during my childhood, as did all the boys I knew? Or was it that now working almost continually with men, I was finding a preference for theoretical rather than applied science? Was this a way to retain my femininity in a male environment? Perhaps I was content with not knowing how a radio or an automobile worked, if that distinguished me as feminine.

While I was choosing physics as my major field of study, I was having no trouble deciding on government as my minor. It is hard to understand why no worries about working in a male field interfered with this choice. The explanation must simply be that in time of war, government meant working to avoid war, and thus something everyone needed to understand and be able to use.

When Radcliffe's Undergraduate Dean discovered that I hadn't taken an introductory physics course in high school or at Harvard, she insisted I do so. Now a senior and feeling superior as an advanced physics student in an all-female course, I was required to register for a course in which a young instructor (I was used to senior professors) presented the usual overview of nineteenth century physics: Newton's laws, optics, acoustics and electricity. Mathematical explanations were avoided in such "introductory" courses, ostensibly to make the subject more accessible to general students. Following this habit, the instructor's presentations included mostly the "what" not the "why" of physical laws, not offering the explanations from atomic theory that I relished. Thinking the class must be both boring and abstruse for its students and not wanting to deprive them of "real" physics, I wanted to declaim, "This isn't physics!" In fact, I rebelled so thoroughly that I earned a "C," my lowest grade in college! Even before the course was over, I started blaming the "facts only" approach of this course for the dearth of Radcliffe girls choosing more science courses. Was this conclusion influenced by my new idea that theory was more "feminine" than practice? But, my negative experience with this course soon had a lasting effect in prompting my devotion to teaching and learning science.

Throughout these years, I was delighted with the collegial life in and around all of my science classes. Our class lab work was usually conducted in teams, and included plenty of chatting, joking and discussion. Questions were developed and answers reinforced collaboratively. I felt fortunate to be spending my afternoons in laboratories with compatible classmates, rather than alone in libraries where my non-science friends spent theirs. After five years of girls' schools, coeducation felt just right! Often the only female in science and math classes, I was simply happy to be doing what the boys were doing. I approached my Harvard professors as I had my father's friends, expecting to respect them and wanting them to respect me. As I became less naïve, I became more self-conscious and remember asking Professor Oldenberg, while in a group of students talking with him, how he felt about having a girl in one of his courses. I liked the objectivity of his answer: "Well, who else would wear a red blazer to class?" I did indeed have a red blazer, sent to me by my mother, who wanted to keep me well dressed. For older students and professors, a girl in class was an intriguing, but not a disturbing, anomaly. Roy Glauber, 2005 Nobel Laureate in physics, enjoys telling me that while he was an undergraduate at Harvard he wanted to know the only females in his physics classes—Winifred

Prince (later a lifelong friend) and me—because we were "attractive and interesting."

When Harvard opened its classrooms to us, Radcliffe girls were accepted much as "Rosie the Riveter" was on factory floors: we filled places left empty by men at war. Harvard welcomed female tuition-paying students to take the places of males now in military service. I recall no sexual bias or harassment, of me or another female, in my Harvard classes. Perhaps I was too young and naïve, too respectful of faculty members and too happy to be in a coed environment to notice biased behavior. After the war, however, gender bias certainly returned as I heard ample complaints from female students during those years. Apparently, women were less welcome in Harvard Yard when sitting in seats wanted by men.

Many pleasant dates with the young Navy recruits and officers in my classes provided my social life. Prompted by our wartime awareness of mortality, several temporary "older brothers" wrote me homesick letters from their naval assignments in the Pacific. I lost track of Ken from physics class, but have great memories of Eddy and his roommate Alex. They often walked me to physics class, calling us the "three musketeers." With such an escort, no wonder I was happy with the subject! Both moved on to distinguished science careers. When Alex wrote about his college career, he said his "real fascination came from learning about atoms and molecules." I felt the same way. As I learned about the structure and behavior of atomic particles, I began to understand the "oddities" of their behaviors and sizes that had first fascinated me in school.

All around me I saw World War II reshape the work of friends, faculty and family. When the U.S. Office of Scientific Research and Development asked my father to direct wartime research on the toxicity of chemical warfare reagents, he and my mother moved, temporarily, to Chicago where the project was based. A biochemist, he was assigned responsibility for assessing the qualities of the nation's supply of poison gas, the very stuff that had threatened his life in World War I. Although still a British subject, he had top security clearance for such work, which he then led out of one of the University of Chicago's squash courts. The "Manhattan Project" for the atomic bomb occupied the adjacent court. It was not my father's style to talk about his feelings or memories, so I could only imagine how it felt to be engaged again in a war, after losing his youth and most young friends in a "War to End All Wars." Often I found him in a chair, doing and saying nothing, just staring into the middle distance. The trauma of his wartime memories, coupled with his English taste for understatement and a "stiff upper lip" left him unwilling, or unwitting, to talk about such feelings with me . . . or anyone else I know.

I spent the summer of 1944 at Radcliffe, sometimes studying while lying in a cold bath to escape the heat! Exhausted after studying at Radcliffe/Harvard for three semesters straight, I took the next semester off, joining my parents in Chicago for a few months during my father's war work there. I moved into a Murphy bed in my parents' small hotel apartment, close to the University of Chicago campus, and can still feel the cold wintry winds from Lake Michigan stinging my bare legs above socks and saddle shoes as I walked across the Midway to the campus bookstore where I held my first paid job as a sales clerk. There I acquired my Social Security number: forever after identifying me as from the state of Illinois.

The summer of 1945 was spent in Woods Hole, celebrating the end of the European war with some sun-and-sea playtime. A call came from the Woods Hole Oceanographic Institution (WHOI) seeking temporary young women workers for measuring work (it was always young women who were sought for such routine jobs) for their ongoing naval research. I responded to the call and took a job for about a month in a lab overlooking Woods Hole's busy and beautiful Great Harbor. My job was measuring the distance between marks of underwater impact recorded on photographic film after research ships launched depth discharges.

Recently reminiscing about war work during his undergraduate years, Roy Glauber, a physics classmate of mine, told me that he was assigned to teach Army Specialized Training Program (ASTP) students during his freshman year. He had been admitted to Harvard in 1942 from the Bronx High School of Science, already having taken some advanced physics. After teaching a class to ASTP students, he found a man "in a suit" (which was to say, not a professor) waiting for him with the offer of a job at Los Alamos National Laboratory. This gentleman was from the National Roster of Scientific Personnel, the government agency managing resources and needs for scientists for a full variety of wartime jobs. He told Roy that he should take the job to "help his country" and did not fail to mention that it would probably warrant a military deferment. Roy took the job, finished his degree after the war and continued to a Ph.D., a professorship, and then the Nobel Prize in Physics in 2005 for his work on quantum optics.

Faculty as well as students disappeared on mysterious assignments. In early 1945, I was sitting and chatting with Professor Philipp Frank on the steps of the Jefferson Physics Laboratory when he asked me if I knew where Professor Bainbridge had gone. Finding I did not know, Professor Frank explained that he had left to work in "Shangri La," which he described to me as "that place in New Mexico where they are trying to split the atom to make a bomb." Thus, I was shocked, but not surprised by news of the Nagasaki and Hiroshima bombs. Colleagues working on nuclear explosives may well have been taken for granted within the physics department, but my only evidence for this assumption is my memory of this conversation. In later years, Roy Glauber explained to me that since physicists working on the Manhattan Project in Los Alamos, New Mexico, knew more about nuclear physics than university physicists, universities competed to hire these "stars" and build physics departments around them. This star culture persists to this day, promoting more competitive and stressful environments in advanced science departments than existed pre-war.

On entering college, amid the difficulties of choosing mathematics or physics as a major, I had chosen a minor in government and joined a student group, the Harvard Post-War Council. Its president, Fred de Hoffman, was so articulate in his opposition to the racially discriminatory poll tax in the South that many of us students followed. I joined the Radcliffe League for Democracy, later becoming its president. I do recall leading our group to join an "anti-poll tax" campaign in partnership with the Harvard Liberal Union. In the late 1940s, some of the organizations recruiting students were suspected of being Communist fronts. With my co-president, Sara Portnoy, later a partner in a distinguished New York City law firm, we visited the office of one of these groups on the second floor of a building on Brattle Street. As soon as we saw a poster on the wall depicting a big Russian bear and a diminutive Uncle Sam repelling the Nazis, Sara and I beat a hasty retreat down the stairs. When my father learned what I was doing, he asked me, because of his sensitive professional position, to "keep your name out of the papers." Otherwise he presented no challenge, except perhaps an intellectual argument, to whatever I was up to.

As president of the Radcliffe League for Democracy I was invited to represent Radcliffe at the first meeting of the United World Federalists in Concord, Massachusetts. Cord Meyer, a wounded war hero who eventually became a high-ranking CIA official, co-founded this organization. It was shortly after atomic bombs had fallen, so I arrived at the meeting full of idealism about how the world must avoid another world war. And yet, as often happens, reality got in the way. Discussion amongst delegates at this first World Federalist meeting centered on their confirming the number of votes to allot each nation. Difficulties in reaching consensus dominated and undermined the proceedings, as comparable issues still do at the United Nations today. Not surprisingly, no agreement on a future voting plan was reached before the meeting adjourned. After the conference, I discovered that Cord Meyer and I were taking Harvard's undergraduate course in constitutional law at the same time. It was surprising to learn that he was also reading the Federalist papers for the first time.

That same semester, in November 1945, *The Radcliffe News* asked me, the only physics major in the senior class, to write an article about the world government meeting and the exploding of the world's first atomic bomb. Here is a portion of what I wrote:

> *If we could see the real value of scientific progress and discovery in its philosophic implications and in its "Way of Life," as Professor Bridgman puts it, we could really be on the way to a more mature social order. There is great danger that the utilitarian aspects of science will be overemphasized by the man in the street. In the future, atomic power can bring us great relief from material wants and struggles, but this technological value must not be thought of as an end in itself.*

I remain abidingly proud of these words, particularly the last sentence. In today's global technology environment, they grow in importance for me every day. Some words in my editorial must have been triggered by a speech by Professor Bridgman (soon a Physics Nobelist) in which he spoke of "ways of life," but, I cannot recall where I got the explicit concept that "technological value must not be thought of as an end in itself." I was foreseeing today's society in which "making" or using progressively newer technological gadgetry is, for many, an "end in itself." Was this idea just born of my greater delight in theoretical than practical ideas, my technological illiteracy growing up as a girl, a bias that technology was more male than female or simply the personal taste that I continued to enjoy for years to come?

My favorite class at Harvard, Philosophy of Physics, started me thinking of science as a process of inquiry, and comparing it to inquiry in other disciplines. The course professor, Philipp Frank, and Albert Einstein had been leaders of the "Vienna Circle," notable for its achievements in developing nuclear physics and the philosophy of logical positivism. In Frank's course, I relished learning of direct relationships between modern science and politics: modern science and the Enlightenment, Newtonian determinism and Marxism, relativity and existentialism. Frank believed that even more important than science's technical applications is its impact on our common-sense picture of the world. Here is another source of my conviction that technological products are not ends in themselves. Frank argued that science is truly a "natural philosophy," as it was called in its earliest days, and further argued that if philosophy is part of science, it should be part and parcel of science instruction. This thought, first absorbed in Frank's Philosophy of Physics course, remains central to my later ambitions for science education. To support his observation that "the central problem in the philosophy of sciences is how we get from common-sense statements to general scientific principles," he quoted Walt Whitman:

> Logic and sermons never convince,
> The damp of the night drives deeper into my soul,
> Only what proves itself to every man and woman is so,
> Only what nobody denies is so.

The five words "what nobody denies is so" remain, for me, the best way to describe science's objective and its achievements. In his 1956 book *The Philosophy of Science*, Frank explored the roles of hypothesis, observation and theory in deriving knowledge "that nobody denies is so." In those days we included with our exam papers stamped postcards that the professor mailed back after recording our grades. On my post-card Philipp Frank wrote: "A+. Radcliffe won this race." There was no sexism in that kind and brilliant man.

Frank's explication of science became explicit for me in discussions with a classmate, Peggy Dorgan, a devoted Roman Catholic. While sitting together at a desk in her room reviewing Thomas Aquinas for an exam in a philosophy class we were taking together, Peggy said to me, "Cecily, isn't it wonderful how Aquinas answers all one's questions?" But Aquinas did not answer mine. I found his arguments embedded in the meaning of the words he used, e.g., "nature," "God" and "man." In science we analyze observations, while, for me, philosophy was mostly analyzing words. I told Peggy that I was happy he answered her ques-tions, but he did not answer mine. Within the year, Peggy left college to join the Carmelite order of nuns, returning years later to finish her degree. We kept in touch for several years, later marveling that despite the differences between our lives, we were learning similar things about life, love and the pursuit of happiness. I was surprised at how well she understood marriage and its issues from her talks with communicants at their private monastery window. Peggy was in her convent reading and listening to communicants while I was busy with urban life as a professional, wife and mother. As Sister Marie Therese, she worked hard for more autonomy and freedom for herself and members of her order, and provided widespread guidance for meditation through her writings and teachings.

At examination time, I relished what I considered my advantage over non-science classmates: a good night's sleep. In physics and chemistry, exam questions include the information needed to solve the problems presented. For problem solving it was neither wise nor necessary to stay up all night to memorize information. We were being examined primarily on our cognitive skills. Later in life, my physical chemist husband told me he often slipped extraneous evidence into an exam question to test a student's ability to distinguish relevant from irrelevant evidence . . . a cognitive skill! My friends in the humanities, however, dealt with large interacting systems, including more "unknowns" than "knowns," and thus did not have the luxury of solving problems that have answers. My father had taught me that to solve equations including "n" unknowns, you need "n" equations: a rare situation in the social sciences. In those days I preferred scientific certainties, while now my tastes run to complex predicaments!

It was in college that I started to blame academic divorce—the "two cultures" divide—between the sciences and the humanities (or the sciences and the arts) on curricular design and attitudes. Scientific information is, too often, presented as a finished product, rather than as stages in scientific inquiry. At the Dalton School, I had first found knowledge presented as a narrative of exciting exploration rather than as a list of required steps. At college, the science curriculum was, and mostly remains, designed as a linear route of required courses. Those who navigate the obstacle course of science courses and their prerequisites become professionals, if not guardians, of an elite temple of powerful and useful knowledge. This practice has long excluded those undergraduate students not already committed to professional science from developing scientific or technological literacy. In contrast, arts and humanities curricula at least welcomed science and engineering students, giving them an opportunity to assimilate their values and interests.

My dismay that interest in scientific literacy was not more widely shared steadily increased during my college years. Particularly, I noticed that the geographic separation on campus between science and arts and humanities buildings reinforced their curricular separation. Dealing with these issues was to come later. My immediate task, as a college senior, was to figure out what I should do next. My classmates were busy reconnecting with men who had been away at war. Nineteen years old and two years younger than my classmates, I had no committed boyfriend coming home from the service, and did not seek to marry at my young age. I well recall how I fitted into the mores of the time by saying to myself it would be nice to be "number two to a great man." For a while, my idea of a "great man" was a foreign correspondent! I can recall no ambition to be "number one" myself, somehow reserving that honor for a male partner. Implicit in this message was my assumption, shared by my friends, that marriage and family has priority over career. For my post-war generation, most saw their first responsibility as helping to put their husbands through medical or law school, assuming that they would then be able to support them financially.

When my now lifelong friend Betty invited me to share a room with her at Saville House, a small residence house, for my senior year, I joined a small group of interesting classmates who had arranged to live there together. Over all my later years, Betty and I shared so much (sons, skiing, science) throughout long lives of close friendship. Living with her in a cohesive, compatible group for my senior year so happily and fortunately told me that I was no longer "different"—I belonged to the Class of 1946. At Saville House, we could share our lives more closely than in a dormitory. Betty and two other members of this group were science majors, which fostered compatibility. At our commencement, I became a lasting close friend of David Ewing, the brother of housemate Barbara Ewing. It was a privilege to also be privy to Barbara's romance with our popular government professor, Paul Ylvisaker, a future Dean of Harvard's School of Education. How well I remember being with Barbara when we retrieved our bicycles after a class in Sever Hall, and found Paul's note on hers: "The owner of this bike is taken." In my last year at college, I was no longer an "outsider"!

Our graduation in June 1946 at Memorial Hall, Harvard's sentimentally beloved, but odd looking building, made history as we were the first Radcliffe class to earn Harvard diplomas co-signed by Harvard and Radcliffe's presidents. Our class certainly was responsible for many "firsts": one joined the first class accepting women at Harvard Medical School and another the first such class at Columbia Law School. I really had no idea about what I wanted to do next. I had a yen to return to England, but my father cited financial reasons for not applying for a fellowship at Cambridge University. Fellowships, he said, would be harder to get in the U.K. than in the U.S. Nor did my parents endorse another item on my "wish" list: a dream of freedom from responsibility expressed in the following words I wrote in a letter home shortly before graduation, when I was clearly tired of studying.

> *I think you understand my point of view now—that one*
> *of the points of my being sped through school so young was*
> *to have a year or two of grace to travel and play around*

with etc., and that now I am through college with the habit of studying all these years I frankly want as much travel and new experience as possible and feel far from mature enough to just change my groove from one sort of study to exactly the same thing again. If I can feel this relieved at being over exams I sincerely wonder whether I have the right attitude for graduate work. On the other hand, I know a job would be far less interesting and educational than graduate work.

Although I had pretty well discounted continuing in physics, my mind was not closed to another science, largely thanks to an unanticipated letter I received during my last semester inviting me to become a Junior Member of the Society of Sigma Xi. I didn't know what Sigma Xi stood for, so I asked a friend, who told me it was science's honor society, comparable to Phi Beta Kappa for the humanities. When she expressed disappointment that she, a biology major, had not been invited, I realized that my physics professors had honored me with their nomination. Their letter said I had shown "a potential for scientific research." These words packed a wallop that lasted a long time to come. I felt that they had handed me an obligation to continue in the sciences. Their honoring me for physics study suggested that, perhaps, it was through contributing to the sciences that I could pay back to society for my privileged education. But should it be in physics?

That discipline then reigned at top of the scientific heap of public attention, as information technology and biological engineering do today. Radar and nuclear fission had turned the tide of the war, and a grateful nation was doling out funding and recognition. Dozens of nuclear physicists, like Roy Glauber, were returning from Los Alamos and military service older, wiser and more highly qualified than I. With so many experienced nuclear physicists swelling academic departments, nuclear physics research would be split up into smaller and smaller pieces of the puzzle of atoms and their nuclei. As Roy had explained, the search for "star" scientists was underway. Was I sufficiently interested in the small details of the big picture of nuclear physics to want to compete? Writing to my parents, I said:

I do want to be in the scientific world of some sort but am still interested in all the sciences. If I concentrate on graduate work for an M.A. in physics, the only courses I have left to take are electromagnetic theory and quantum physics. I have taken everything else in nuclear physics. The average age of my classmates is now 26. I am by far the youngest. I feel I would be a better contributor to graduate work if I were older and more on a level with my fellow classmates . . . . Physics has only recently become such an important field . . . I know enough about the process of its development to know that I do not think it would be interesting for me to do research in nuclear physics. In a way it seems to be too far ahead of itself. Paradoxically, it seems less exciting because it has progressed so far to its own limits.

Perhaps nuclear physics had already progressed far beyond its own limits, but I certainly had not. Explorations in the sciences, in the arts and in teaching and learning lay ahead. The best delights of life and love were not yet even dreamed of.

3

A Minority at MIT

Scientific methodology today is based on generating hypotheses and testing them to see if they can be falsified; indeed this methodology is what distinguishes science from other fields of human inquiry.
—U.S. Supreme Court, U.S. Supreme Court, 1993,
quoting Sir Karl Popper

In a darkened room, the moving images on the screen took my breath away. Riveted, I watched cell membranes breaking apart and resealing, mitotic spindles physically splitting chromosomes, and then, one cell becoming two. It was the summer of 1946, and I was visiting my father at the National Academy of Sciences, viewing with him and his colleagues a black-and-white film just received from scientists in post-war Germany. This film presented to U.S. scientists the highest magnification view of dividing living cells yet developed, and it changed my life.

I was in Washington exploring job possibilities for a 19-year-old brand new female Harvard A.B. in physics. While memories of this vision of dividing cells have lasted a lifetime, memories of my job interviews have not. Despite my Harvard degree, employers considered me, not yet 20 years old, too young to hire. I was not disappointed because the jobs appeared clerical and I could hardly type. With this news, I quickly gave up the glamorous appeal of the option of sharing a house with some Radcliffe graduates in Washington, an option very attractive to us raw college graduates in those early post-war days.

Following job interviews at places like the Office of Scientific Personnel and the Association of Atomic Scientists, I visited my father at his elegant office in the monumental white National Academy of

Sciences building dominating Constitution Avenue. He was back in Washington after leading the first U.S. team to review bomb damage at Hiroshima and Nagasaki, as Chair of the Academy's National Research Council, the operating arm of the National Academies of Science and Engineering. His responsibilities encompassed the acquisition and dissemination of knowledge in matters involving science, engineering, technology and health to improve national decision-making, public understanding and public policy.

The black-and-white images shown in my father's office that day gave me a stunning vision of a frontier in biology about which, until then, I had known nothing. This first viewing of biological cells dividing was the tipping point that shifted my scientific curiosity from invisible atoms to microscopically visible living cells, from mathematical simulations of the invisible to microscopy images making the invisible visible. My attention moved away from the mathematical and physical constructs I knew in physics ("restless particles") to biology's more lively constructs of living things. I started wondering whether I should work on things more "human" than nuclear particles. After our film viewing, I listened to biologists in the audience expressing excitement over the advanced technology that could record living cells at such high magnification. Thus, I was hearing talk of applying new physical tools to the study of biology. While new technologies imaging electricity had previously left me cold, I was now excited about technologies imaging living things. That biologists at MIT were using new physical tools from wartime research to explore life sounded important and interesting. Thus, I paid attention when my father told me that MIT had started a new biology department to concentrate on applying physics to biology. Could this be a place where I could apply the math and physics I knew to "human" territories?

To learn more, one summer morning in 1946 I took the short train ride from Woods Hole to Boston to visit MIT. Although MIT was Harvard's next-door neighbor, I had, until then, known little about it and had never entered its doors. I liked the white stone profile it presented when viewed from the Charles River, with its gigantic central dome providing a striking contrast to the soft profile of Harvard's nearby collection of smaller brick colonial buildings and Boston's red brick row houses on the other side of the river. During my interview in MIT's Physical Biology Department, I learned that they would welcome a student who had studied math and physics, even though she had never, in either school or college, studied biology.

On my return to Woods Hole that night with this good news, I found my father impressed and surprised by the success of my interview. His interest made it easy for me to decide to commit to graduate school at MIT, although, at the time, it did feel that I was just taking the "path of least resistance" in doing what my father knew and liked. But I was happy to return to Cambridge, even if it was the one in Massachusetts, not England! Several college friends, male and female, would be there, as would my new friend, Dave Ewing, whom I had met when he visited his sister, Barbara, for Radcliffe's commencement. We quickly started a correspondence so I knew that he would be attending Harvard Law School, and I could look forward to his company.

That summer in Woods Hole was a carefree one, celebrating the end of wartime with friends and neighbors, who had just returned from military service, were in their late teens like myself or were in their early twenties. We spent our days together on beaches and tennis courts, with evenings in each other's homes, playing charades, making music or, for me, just learning about grown-up partying. I joined a local amateur theater group, called the Penzance Players and, maybe thanks to my English accent, was offered the part originally taken by Gertrude Lawrence in Noel Coward's *Tonight at 8:30*. To this day, this group of friends identifies me as the actress I was then. After this brief theatrical excitement, I was off to MIT in September 1946, with financial support from a National Institutes of Health fellowship the department arranged for me.

The Physical Biology Department (the only biology department at MIT in those days) was on the third floor of MIT's main building, directly under the Institute's dome. A wide staircase leads up to the department's labs and offices. Every time I visit MIT and climb this staircase, I recall the feelings of happiness, comfort and belonging to something of value that I always felt climbing up to the biology department. I felt proud to be at MIT, and comfortable and involved with the work, the life and the people there. I relished my new independence, alternating studying and lab work with Boston Symphony concerts, theater, dinners out with Dave and other friends and ski weekends with the MIT Outing Club. I enjoyed the freedom of independent living together with the collegiality of laboratory life and friendships with students and professors. Indeed, I was very happy at MIT for the three years I spent there finishing my studies and completing my research.

My department was small, but it was a national leader in moving biology into the new era of molecular and physical biology. I don't remember competition or stress among us few students—only confidence and satisfaction in using new technological tools to explore small structures inside biological cells. There was a friendly culture with a more personalized approach than I had found in large undergraduate classes. As in college, I particularly remember experiences with didactic teaching, such as the occasion when an engineering professor introduced a fundamental law by saying briskly, "I don't have time to go into why this law is true. All you need to know is that it works." Clearly, what I loved about my graduate studies was that we were encouraged to try to figure out why things behaved as they did.

MIT had a residential building for male graduate students, but no housing for women. Two Radcliffe graduates invited me to share their apartment on Bowdoin Street in Cambridge, adjacent to the Radcliffe Quad. As we settled in, I was adjusting well to academic work and an easy social life with Dave, while they were struggling with the unfriendly rigors of medical school and did not have a "Dave" in their lives. They did, however, have time to notice my housekeeping, and summoned me for a talk: "Your desk is always tidy but you never sweep under the bed." I did try to mend my ways, and when they found better accommodation near their medical school, I found a room in a house on Fenway Park, closer to MIT. I shared this with an art student, Joyce, who would later become my housemate on Marlborough Street. She and I each had a bedroom and shared a living room large enough to house, temporarily, a larger-than-life clay sculpture belonging to one of Joyce's classmates. My hours at home were spent studying at my desk overlooking the roofs of neighboring attached houses, my only distraction there being the lives and loves of the pigeons on the rooftops. During my last year at MIT, I lived in similar quarters within Harvard's campus, on Mount Auburn Street, taking the Mass Avenue streetcar to MIT. When my father, who was providing living expenses, asked how much money I needed for food, I said $10 a week would be fine because I could count on being invited out for dinner by boyfriends once a week. His response was, "Graft, that's what it is: graft."

Some former classmates remember me as the sole, or rare, "coed" in their class. Recently chatting with Dr. Murray Gell-Mann, 1969 Nobel Prize winner in physics, a graduate student in that subject who remembered sharing some studies with me, I was surprised when he told me, "All the boys were in love with you." I don't believe him—but would have enjoyed knowing this charming gentleman and stunning scientist then. My classes were filled with young men. The only place in which to meet other MIT women was the Margaret Cheney Room, a spacious room and kitchen provided by alumnae for women students. The kitchen was great for heating canned soup and making a sandwich while the lounge offered some comfort and privacy. It meant a lot to us few women that an alumna and the Institute had funded this space for us. I was engaged by the submicroscopic structures of nerves and other tissues, not by how I was treated as a female. Physical Biology was a new and small department, with few graduate students, so our classes were friendly and informal, and the department was already in a dominant position in the new disciplines of molecular and physical biology.

When I was so very often asked what it was like to be among the small minority of female students at MIT, my easy answer used to be that the ratio of 80 women to 5000 men was good news for an eligible female. The more complete response is that I did not feel conspicuous in my department. Frank Schmitt, and another professor, Irwin Sizer, created a working environment that was cheerful, friendly and accepting to *all* students, male and female. Both were fine scientists, humanists and teachers who maintained a happy tribe of students and professors, one to which I felt proud to belong. The faculty included one female scientist, while I was the only female grad student for most of my time there. Nineteen years old when I arrived, I was also the youngest graduate student in the department. Since I recall no oppressive competition or stress or evident bias while I was there, it is important to recall that, through Woods Hole and visits to my father's labs, I was already familiar and comfortable with academic climates and attitudes. I could recognize difficulties experienced by those not having such a family friendly introduction to academic life. I remember another female student complaining that a professor had not said "hello" to her in the corridor that day. Familiar with busy absorbed professors moving around corridors, I was surprised that she should, routinely, expect a "hello." Confident and happy with new tools to play with and biological forms and functions to explore, I felt "at home" in an academic culture. Often, Dr. Sizer invited us to bring our sandwiches to his lab at lunchtime, where we could celebrate a birthday or a job appointment, with a little champagne for all, served in a glass laboratory beaker. Then, as now, my idea of a good party!

Dr. Schmitt was recognized globally for his leadership in high magnification studies of nerve cell structure. His extroverted personality and energetic teaching epitomized the style of professors I most enjoy: those who communicate information and ideas energetically and interactively with others. His research focused on the giant axon of the squid, a nerve so large it could be dissected, measured and analyzed by eye. It runs the whole length of the squid's body and is fifty times wider than any human nerve fiber. One assumes that this powerful nerve allowed the squid a quick getaway from predators! To this day, the squid continues to be a model for teaching and research on nerve structure and function. Biological studies are often advanced by felicitous choices of animal models to work with: the drosophila fly, the zebra fish and mice are other examples of biological models abundantly used for research.

On admission to MIT, I was told not to "bother" with a master's degree but to go straight ahead to a doctorate. This required enrolling in basic biology courses I had not yet taken and then conducting an original research investigation with the leadership and counsel of the professor who would be my thesis adviser. The relationship between a graduate student and his or her adviser should be mutually beneficial. The student's project will contribute information to the professor's work, while the professor will contribute experience and guidance to the student's project. As the only professor whose work required advanced math and physics, Dr. Richard Bear was assigned to be my thesis advisor. A devoted and modest scientist loving order in all things, he was committed to what he called "true scholarship and true morality." His approach to science was evident when he wrote that he found "order among facts a very satisfying thing." He was generous and collaborative. However, his trust in me was sorely tried the day he asked me to "ground" a wire while we working on high voltage equipment. When my response made it clear I didn't know what "grounding" meant or how to do it, his face changed and he moved with unaccustomed speed to ground that wire! He published our experimental results in the premier journal for scientific work, *Nature*, twice designating me as co-author, an unusual honor for a Ph.D. student.

With no biology courses yet in my resume, I took every course offered by the department, particularly enjoying Embryology. It amplified the meager sex education I brought to MIT and taught me lots more than I had known about human fertilization and reproduction. Through the famous "Root" embryo studies, I learned how nature protects our species: fertilized eggs that grow to include "mistakes" or deficiencies are ejected through miscarriages. This piece of knowledge prompted my decision that life begins at birth. I became entranced by histology—how cells are structured and organized in biological organs. During my daily walk to MIT over the bridge across the Charles River, I sometimes compared patterns created on the river's surface by the interaction of waves, wind, oil and boats with the patterns of cells in the organs I was studying. Throughout nature, the forms and the functions of biological cells are intimately related. Information about a cell's internal structure leads to increased understanding of how cells organize themselves internally, how they join with others to form tissues and how tissues perform the functions of the organs within which they are embedded. Structures within and between cells are still my favorite topics in biology.

My only disappointing MIT class was an introductory course in physical chemistry (taught in the engineering department) where I found more of the didactic teaching that had troubled me in Harvard's introductory physics. Once again I was shocked to hear a professor say, "I don't have time to go into why this law works." Why, I wondered angrily, should students be asked to learn a law without understanding the theory behind it? This professor went on to say, "All you need to know is that when you have a boiler with pressure 'P' and volume 'V,' you can calculate the temperature of the gas inside with the equation $PV=nRT$." As the only female in a large class of undergraduate engineering students, none of whom I knew, I tried to be inconspicuous and sit in the back row. Never forgetting my boarding school advice not to be "bumptious," I kept my anger at his teaching to myself. But

I could be stubborn! With my anti-chemistry attitudes reinforced by this course, I did not register for two chemistry courses required of all biology graduate students: quantitative and qualitative chemical analysis. Not until my last semester did my professor discover them missing from my record. This forced him to get special permission to excuse me from these courses that taught the analytical skills then required to identify and measure chemical content. Luckily for me, I never needed these skills for my thesis or later research.

I do not regret missing courses in quantitative and qualitative chemical analysis, but I do regret my antipathy to working with live animals, thereby missing so much of what is now called "organismic" (whole body) biology. Growing up without any pets, I felt insecure around dogs and sorry for their being stuck with people rather than other dogs. Knowing so little about animals, I thought we should be kind to them and let them live free in the wild with their own animal companions, far from the interference of human beings. I vividly remember feeling sorry for the horse that was forced to keep me on his back during my riding lessons. Did I have a right to sit on his back, rather than him sitting on mine? Apparently no one had told me that humans domesticated some animals centuries ago. This antipathy to hurting animals transferred to my choosing not to work with small live animals, but rather depending upon the kindness of classmates (always male) to kill mice or frogs for me if necessary for class work. Illogically, I was perfectly happy dissecting dead animals. Living plants were okay to work on because I did not think they felt pain.

Memories of graduate school include recollections of hours spent calculating with a slide rule. Before calculators and computers, the only tools available for quantitative work were charts and tables in reference books, mechanical calculators—and slide rules. Multiplying, dividing and doing trigonometric calculations with slide rules is a "hands-on" activity: its calculations are visually and tangibly evident on the rule itself. I bought a good second-hand slide rule from a classmate for $20, a considerable sum in those days, and wore it on my belt, in its elegant leather case, to show the world that I belonged to a scientific tribe. For sentimental reasons, I did save it, but by the time my sons grew up, they had no use for it. Electronic calculators had become the way to go. Recently, I suggested that slide rules should be among the stage props for the play *Photograph 51*, about Rosalind Franklin's role in DNA research, and lent the theater company my old slide rule. Thus, appropriately, it ended its life with a stint on stage.

Dr. Bear's specialty was using the tool of X-ray diffraction, often identified as X-ray crystallography—the study of the structure of crystals. Light can be focused to create images, but X-rays cannot. In the early 1900s in England, W.L. Bragg found a way to use the diffraction, not the focusing, of X-rays to reveal structure in these arrays. If there is an extremely regular structure (e.g., crystalline) at atomic levels, X-rays passing through it will be diffracted into patterns that can be recorded on photographic film. Measuring the angle and position of the diffracted rays, X-ray crystallographers can deduce how atoms and molecules are arranged. Initially, Bragg used this technique for chemical analyses and for determining how atoms are arranged within crystals. Its first biological triumph was identifying the crystalline structure of penicillin, thus enabling its mass production for saving lives in World War II. A following triumph was when Francis Crick and James Watson used it to reveal the double helical structure of DNA.

Had I had gone to Cambridge University, as I had dreamed, I would have been there when Crick and Watson started their X-ray diffraction studies together at the Cavendish Labs. Later, I did visit the Cavendish labs to meet with Hugh Huxley, then a graduate student there. He and I were busy studying the submicroscopic structure of muscles, he in England's Cambridge, and I in America's. Coincidentally, while I was in graduate school, my college roommate, Betty Weichel, had become a technical expert working with several prominent crystallographers, including a number of women. Women were among crystallography's earliest pioneers, perhaps encouraged by the attitude and egalitarian collaborative culture Bragg and J. D. Bernal promoted in their laboratories. Crystallography produced two Nobel Laureates and one of the first two women elected to Britain's Royal Society.

Dr. Bear was concentrating on the structure of the muscle protein myosin, the protein responsible for muscular contraction. Other researchers had identified a couple of proteins within muscle fibers, but in the late 1940s no muscle proteins had yet been isolated in fibrous form. Only specimens such as crystals, already ordered or crystalline in structure, are susceptible to analysis by X-ray diffraction. Three years later, Francis Crick and Jim Watson were successful in their analysis because they had an excellent fibrous form of DNA, prepared by their colleague Rosalind Franklin, to work with. With no such preparation available for muscle, Bear decided to work on the protein in situ, that is to say, as it is situated in nature. He chose the adductor muscle holding clams together because this tissue, a smaller, narrower version of the scallop we eat, is close to 100 percent aligned muscle fiber. Bear had designed and built a special "slit" structure through which the X-rays passed before penetrating the clam muscle. By pulling the clamshells apart without breaking them (my job), we maximized the longitudinal alignment of muscle fibers. Next, we used the high-tech tool of a rubber band (!!) to clamp the shells together. I then passed an X–ray beam through the muscle still attached to the shell for many days, thereby exposing photographic film at the other end of the X-ray path. Sometimes our exposures lasted a week or two—enabling this student to take off for a quick trip to the beach!

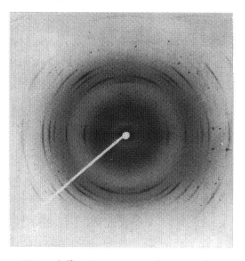

X-ray diffraction pattern, clam muscle,
Nature 168, 1951

I traveled by subway to Boston's fish market to obtain our clams and became quite adept at opening them to a certain point before binding the shells with a rubber band. The photos I obtained had clear similarities to Rosalind Franklin's now famous "Photograph 51," looking similar to the photograph on which my Ph.D. thesis results were built.

"Using the tool of X-ray diffraction, what can we learn about the molecular structure of clam adductor muscle?" This was the question my Ph.D. dissertation was designed to answer. As a first step, I had to learn from reading scientific journals what other scientists had already discovered about muscle biology and chemistry. My analysis had to build on information already established. Then, I measured patterns of and distances between spots produced on photographic film after X-rays passed through the muscle. My job was to try to figure out, mathematically, what molecular structure could have produced them. We started with our best hypothesis for this structure, and then my time was spent on completing the following mathematical analysis to see if it could support this hypothesis. Working through this analysis with differential equations, I did find a rectilinear hypothesis that worked. Sadly, I did not explore the helical hypothesis that, years later, turned out to be the winning one. My professor had said, "Don't bother to look at the helical model. I am sure it is not a helix." He had very good reasons for saying this, but three years later, Crick and Watson did try a helical model in their study of DNA structure, and, triumphantly, it worked! The model structure that Bear and I came up with for the clam's muscle protein was rectilinear, not helical. It was published in the journal *Nature* in 1951, and not refuted until a couple of decades later when, using improved tools and technique, it was replaced by a helical model. Dr. Bear's failure to pursue a helical hypothesis was unlucky, but not bad science. Our result was a reasonable one based on what was known at the time. Although our rectilinear hypothesis was later disproved, our procedures and analyses utilized good science and mathematics, and helped lead those who followed to the ultimately successful structure: a familiar story of scientific discovery.

Discovery in science is directly dependent on the capacity of the tools available, the quality of the questions asked, and the hypotheses chosen. The increased power of X-ray diffraction yielded new data, which could answer new questions and prompt new hypotheses to test. More often than not, the new observations made by the new tool may disprove the initial hypothesis. Here, the words of my former professor, Philipp Frank, are appropriate, "Science is like a detective story. All the facts confirm a certain hypothesis, but in the end the right one may be a completely different one." Following our work and that of Crick and Watson, others continued to develop and test hypotheses for protein structure. A fit between the guessed structure and the diffraction pattern actually observed was considered evidence that the hypothesized structures could be the actual structures within the specimen. The DNA double helix model reported from the Cavendish Laboratory in Cambridge, England, in 1953, was fully accepted after the model was supported by other established laboratory techniques. Two independent investigators, Meselson and Stahl, then created and performed an experiment that confirmed the Crick/Watson hypothesis. Bingo! Quoting Professor Frank again, it became the "truth that no one can deny." It also fits Andrei Sakharov's view of hypotheses, so beautifully expressed in words during a talk I heard at Rockefeller University, "When scientists fight, their hypotheses die in their stead."

In 1948, two years after I had joined the biology department at MIT, I was asked to give a departmental seminar entitled "Present Status of X-Ray Diffraction Studies of Muscle." I remember feeling totally inept, but later heard some praise for my use of a fresh approach. After speaking with Dr. Schmitt about my seminar, my father commented, "From the general tenor of his remarks, I gather that your descent upon MIT has not passed without creating something of a stir. It would appear that you are not quite in the traditional mold of a graduate. Anyway he is impressed. He liked your way of conducting the seminar, which he acknowledged was rather an unfair assignment. He thought that your technique of firing salvos of questions a singularly clever device."

Two months later, I sat for my major Ph.D. examination: a written test to assess what I had learned over the past two years of course work. In a copy I kept of this exam and some notes I made, I apparently figured out that each of the department's professors contributed one question. My own advisor asked, "What kinds of information can be drawn from X-ray diffraction studies? What is the ultimate limitation of the method?" The question I chose not to answer was about "modern concepts of gene action and structure," a topic that did not enter required biology curricula until a few years later, and one in which my knowledge remains limited!

This was also the time I decided I should become an American citizen. My tuition was paid by a fellowship from the National Institutes of Health, so I decided that, to be fair, I should join the nation that was supporting me. I filed my application in Boston and was duly sworn in. As I passed through a line for my papers to be signed, the (Irish!) clerk said, "Oh, you're from England. We don't get many of you, but when we do, you make the best citizens!" Quickly following my lead, my parents made their own applications at about this time.

Biology's "big ideas" were turning out to be even more exciting than those I had loved in physics. Indeed, they would remain useful to me in virtually all my endeavors for years to come. Most often, meeting and knowing people responsible for these big ideas triggered my own fascination with thinking at philosophic levels. At MIT, this was possible when distinguished scientists visiting Dr. Schmitt then met and talked with us graduate students. Vivid memories of one Nobel Laureate, Chandrasekhar V. Raman, are of the rubies and emeralds he pulled out of his long flowing Indian robes while talking with me about crystallography. It did seem appropriate for a world-famous Indian crystallographer to carry precious stones in his robes! Raman spectroscopy, named for him, is a very familiar tool today, particularly in large bioengineering enterprises where it helps identify the chemistry of gases and liquids. Tiny Raman spectroscopes are also invaluable for use under the ocean, on earth and in space. Just as today's tiny computers evolved from massive, factory-sized machines at MIT, so tiny spectroscopes evolved from the initial room-size MIT spectroscope that Raman proudly showed me. His delight in aesthetic as well as intellectual ideas and imagination within his work became clear as he talked about his machine with me.

At around this time, I was invited to a private home in Cambridge to hear J.D. Bernal address a small group. Born in Ireland, Bernal was educated in England and became famous not only for his leadership in the earliest work on protein crystal structures but also for his social activism. Politically, he had long been attracted to socialism and was generally considered to be a Marxist. Scientifically, he followed Bragg's leadership in X-ray crystallography. His studies of protein crystals introduced the world to the molecular structures underlying living things: the molecular structures I was exploring at the time. In a living room gathering, Bernal spoke about his social philosophy and presented a design for a town that would fit his ideology. In his design, he illuminated where the police station, the school, the homes and the businesses should be placed. I recall asking the question, "What if people do not want to live where they are assigned?" I do not recall his answer! Once again, I was delighted to hear a scientist exhibit his interest in social theory and practice.

In preparation for the visit of Erwin Schrödinger, 1933 Nobelist in physics, MIT students were encouraged to read his beautiful little book, *What is Life?* In concert with the orientation of Frank Schmitt and our department, Schrödinger sought to bring the wisdom and knowledge of quantum physics to an understanding of the biology of life. His 1944 book opens with the question, "How can the events in space and time which take place within the spatial boundary of a living organism be accounted for by physics and chemistry?" Before the roles of DNA and RNA were even guessed, he posited an "aperiodic crystal" *that contained genetic information in its molecular configuration.* These words have long been credited with stimulating subsequent discovery of genetic/molecular relationships in DNA—and, thereby, attention to molecular configurations in all investigations of normal and abnormal cancer cells. Sitting on the floor near where he sat talking, I asked a question about cancer. He held up one hand and said, "When we know why my finger stopped growing here, we will know something about cancer." Seeking molecular and structural answers to why and how a finger, or a cancer, stops or starts growing would govern the next ten years of my professional life.

4

From Laboratories to Home

*Others (women) in love with their science and doing great
work leave because of inhospitable workplaces and prejudice . . . in the evaluation of their talent.*
—*Nancy Hopkins, MIT, Study on
Women Faculty in Science, 1999*

BY THE FALL OF 1949, I had completed my required courses
and collected experimental data for my research report. All I had
left to do to earn my Ph.D. was to write up this report. I have long been
puzzled why I decided to return to my parents' home in New York to
do this writing. Fatigue with study and lack of financial support were
certainly among the reasons. My fellowship was over, and my father
likely did not want to keep paying for room and board. Maybe I was
simply tired of studying and living uncomfortably in my rented room
with its hotplate kitchen, and no boyfriends were urging me to stay in
Cambridge. I remain puzzled that the two most important men in my
life, my father and my professor, did not encourage me to find a way to
continue my research. Dr. Bear was proud of my work, later including
me as a co-author of the three papers in which he published our results in *Nature*. The Cavendish labs in England were now a stellar team
engaged in X-ray crystallography. Why did neither he nor my father
suggest I apply for a fellowship there? Why didn't I suggest it to myself?
Why didn't my father, loving science research as he did, urge me to stay
around laboratories rather than return home, geographically separating
myself from MIT? Would they have advised a son or male student differently? Would I have made a different decision had I been male?

Letters from my mother were trying to bring me home with the consistent, albeit subtle message, "Come home, your father needs you." It wasn't until Father did leave home, as soon as I married two years later, that I realized my mother hoped that my moving home would forestall his exit. How often I have wondered how differently my life would have turned out had I moved to Cambridge, England, rather than return to New York, where all-consuming family responsibilities soon took over my future. Although creating my own family soon encompassed the happiest and most worthwhile times of my life, I still wish they could have been preceded by a couple of years of freedom to rest and explore before taking on the extensive family responsibilities that came so soon.

Living at home at age twenty-two, especially with tension between my parents, was not the best idea, but I did finish writing up my research report, and thus qualified for my Ph.D. My mother was hoping I would find a husband in Manhattan while I tried a couple of inconsequential interviews for jobs in science writing. Happily, my father's friend, the founder and president of the Sloan-Kettering Institute for Cancer Research (SKI), Cornelius P. Rhoads, well-known as "Dusty," saved the day by offering me an administrative job. Rhoads and my father had worked together on the toxicity of wartime chemical agents, namely poison gases. One such agent was mustard gas, which had revealed some specifically anti-cancer toxicity. With his vigorous personality and mind, Dusty successfully parlayed this information into creating an institute dedicated to treating cancer. A tall, handsome, charming extrovert with a brilliant mind and compelling personality, Rhoads assembled a spectrum of scientific and medical researchers on Manhattan's East 68th Street, in a building designed to meet the needs of cancer research and medical care. He named his new institute for its major donors, Alfred P. Sloan and Charles Kettering.

Dr. Rhoads offered me a position as an assistant to a leading virologist at the Institute, Dr. Alice Moore. I grabbed this opportunity as a job through which I could earn some money, alleviate the boredom of thesis writing and explore work that a Ph.D. would qualify me for. Dr. Moore was studying new evidence that encephalitis viruses could selectively kill cancer cells. While she was investigating viruses as *killers* of cancer cells, other biologists at the adjacent Rockefeller Institute, and elsewhere, were exploring viruses as *causes* of cancer. It was a bellwether time for the exploration of viruses, as well as of cancer. And, it led me to productive and engrossing research.

After a winter of working part-time at Sloan-Kettering and part-time at home, my Ph.D. dissertation was finished, reviewed, and approved, and just in time for MIT's 1950 commencement ceremonies. Mission accomplished! Four years was a speedy time in which to finish a Ph.D., even in those days. That I was Dr. Bear's only graduate student must have hastened the process. I still cherish the Ph.D. hood MIT gave to those who attended commencement. In reporting on this grandiose yearly event, with guests and graduates filling all the institute's space outdoors, under its dome and along the Charles River, *The Boston Traveler* featured a photo of the seven female graduates awarded degrees that day. Four earned master's degrees, and just three of us were awarded doctorates. Apart from this photo, and one of me with my mother, I have few memories of this graduation. Ceremonies marking life's milestones are seldom as memorable as are the experiences leading up to them!

New Ph.D. Cecily Cannan and her mother, Catherine Cannan, 1950

After graduation and a celebratory weekend in Woods Hole, I was back at Sloan-Kettering with my Ph.D. An urge for research had returned when the Institute acquired its first electron microscope and I was the only one around interested in using it. Although I had never used this machine at MIT, I was curious, and with a technician's help, soon learned to operate it. Thus began my eight-year career exploring the structure of biological cells. I soon became Sloan-Kettering Institute's first, and for a while only, electron microscopist.

The move to Sloan-Kettering was remarkably fortuitous. It led to good work with good people in a happy and productive scientific and medical environment. The fascination with biological structures that began in those years has lasted a lifetime. Sloan-Kettering Institute (SKI) also introduced me to my husband. While the electron microscope was redirecting my professional work, an unexpected phone call redirected my personal life. Henry Selby (Hank), a resident doctor in radiology at Memorial Hospital adjacent to and affiliated with SKI, phoned to say he would like to meet me, so could I suggest someone who could introduce us. He had been next to me in the cafeteria line at lunch that day, and had learned my name from the cashier. We started dating. Through Hank's uncle, prominent in New York financial and social circles, I was initiated into a level of New York night life until then completely unknown to me. Dates at The 21 Club, El Morocco and at his relative's elegant townhouse then followed in quick succession. He picked me up in his car at my parents' apartment each morning to drive me to work: a welcome luxury. Nine years my senior, he impressed me with his sophistication and experience with the outside world, and with his wit and appreciation of my work.

Those were exciting times. I was spending evenings with a delightful escort in glamorous, affluent New York style, and days peering down a microscope into the insides of cells. One day, when Hank met my train at Grand Central after I spent a skiing weekend with some Woods Hole friends, he said: "I know you're not ready to get married, but I want to marry you. Just let me know when you are ready." The meeting of two white-coated workers in a hospital had turned into a romance between an eager, curious young woman and an adventurous, responsible physician. In April 1951, I said yes. Hank suggested we shop in New York's Canal district for an engagement ring. We invested both our savings in a beautiful three-carat diamond ring we unearthed at a discount jeweler. Investing so much of one's resources in a ring was a new experience for both of us, but we considered it an appropriate celebration of my husband's new appointment at Memorial Hospital as well as our marriage. With this ring and an article in *The New York*

Times we were officially engaged, and soon married in my parents' apartment. Happy times were ahead. I believed I would no longer be lonely. I belonged: to a loved and good husband, to a social group of young marrieds, to a successful and distinguished institution and to a community of clinical and research workers. Sloan-Kettering became Memorial Sloan-Kettering Cancer Center, and, soon, integral to our family. Over the years ahead, our eldest son was elected a trustee of the Memorial Sloan-Kettering Cancer Center, and his son subsequently spent some years there as a Research Fellow.

An additional responsibility was soon added to my marriage. After my father left for Washington and my parents divorced, my mother's care became my sole responsibility for the next 34 years—there were no siblings or relatives in the U.S. to share it with. My mother never forgave my father for leaving, so, for fear of further hurting her, I did not name a son Keith, as I would have loved to. However, my love for my father survived. I admired and respected his good works: as a devoted researcher and teacher, helpful committee member, eloquent speaker and lover of poetry and theater… a modest but effective mover and shaker in the world of science and its teaching, policies and institutions. He moved to Washington, DC, while my mother moved to an apartment near us, becoming a close member of our family.

For our honeymoon we enjoyed a brilliant European trip with visits to Rome, Rapallo and Florence. The history learned and aesthetics absorbed in this trip were stunning new experiences for me. We stopped off in London before traveling home so I could visit Cambridge to meet Hugh Huxley, whose studies of muscle in Cambridge, U.K., paralleled mine in Cambridge, U.S. Our friendship blossomed later when he and his wife became good friends of mine in Woods Hole. My job qualified us for a small two-bedroom apartment in a nearby building owned by the Memorial Sloan-Kettering Cancer Institute. As husband and wife, we were now working in the same hospital complex: one of us studying the microscopic structure of human cells, and the other studying macroscopic views of the human body. Following his residency, Hank was appointed Attending Radiologist, a position he held for the rest of his working life. Our Saturday nights were spent socializing with other young doctors and their wives at parties where I relished talking medicine with the doctors. Soon my white lab coat became a maternity garment. Our first son, Norman, was born in April 1952, followed within three years by his brothers, Bill and Russell. As I have often told them, my sons were, and remain, the best part of my life.

My white lab coat did not hide my pregnant figure from the scrutiny of the chief surgeon, a leader in radical cancer surgery, Dr. Brunschwig. Standing with a crowd waiting for an elevator one day, he yelled, loud enough for everyone to hear, "Cecily, you need a maternity girdle!" He was right. Its support helped me through three pregnancies, two of which birthed nine-pound babies. Home and work meshed comfortably during those early years, as the Institute's management provided time off when I requested it for baby and child care. My mother, now living alone, pitched in as a very helpful and beloved grandmother. She was jolly and lenient with the boys, laying on them none of the discipline and pressures that marked my young years. She was always available to take them to the park, to pick them up from classes, to visit them at home, and to host them in her Woods Hole cottage when Hank and I went on a couple of trips without them. My sons were very fond of her, and one of my granddaughters carries her name: Katie.

I never considered giving up research. It offered the best way I knew to pay society back for all my educational privileges. I chose to study the nature of cancer, adding some pieces to the jigsaw puzzle of cancer therapy, as my way to contribute to society. With no hesitation, I employed nursemaids and housekeepers to help me run our home. In those early post-war years, well-educated European young women sought post-war travel in the U.S. and were available as mother's helpers and nannies. They spoke good English and were well prepared to be thoughtful caretakers and companions for our sons. Mother was also a helpful part of the team. Young as I was, and unschooled in any other field of learning or doing, my commitment to helping both medicine and our family budget maintained my resolve to continue my professional career. As my husband was just starting his professional medical practice, his salary could not cover all our expenses. My salary helped and soon left enough to buy a house for our young family. My husband said he was glad I worked because I was as tired as he was at the end of the day and didn't want to be bothered with talking about trivia. Busy most nights of the week with social and professional activities, my husband's weekends were his time with the boys. Once our sons started school, I was their full-time caregiver, homework-sharer, and story-listener.

Having grown up without siblings or cousins, I had no experience with small children prior to having my own. But I learned as I went along and adored all the time I had with them. Certainly, there were trying times dealing with arguments between three vigorous boys, each with a strong streak of independence. The word "independent" appeared regularly in each boy's report card! Luckily, we were all blessed with good health, free of medical emergencies in the early years. Always delighted with the unexpected, I remember visiting the kindergarten class of my youngest son, Russell, to discover two bean sprouts growing valiantly in his Dixie cup. Had Russell super germinating powers or had he stealthily slipped two, rather than just one, seed into the soil? Either act would be typical of Russell's originality and independence. When my eldest son, Norman, stepped down from the stage during a class vocal performance, I worried he was misbehaving, only to discover he had been given the honor of taking the baton to lead the class, certainly foreshadowing his lifetime of leadership. His brother, Bill, arrived home one night during his senior year in high school carrying a mandolin he had made in shop class, saying, "This was my best day in school—ever." His delight with working with his hands and making something tangible reminded me of John Dewey's mantra, "Learn by doing." With his creative and aesthetic bent, he started a music group in the eighth grade. He called it the "Sylabills," and I enjoyed driving the group around to its concerts. The evening of one of the keystone events of our generation, our man walking on the Moon, I was in the kitchen with Russell, then a small child. I said, "Surprise! A man has just landed on the Moon." He ran out the kitchen door to look up at the Moon to see! Although my relationship with my husband failed to grow and deepen over time, I was extremely happy with family life during these years and treasure all memories.

I particularly admired the leadership of Dr. Rhoads. With his mix of physical and intellectual energy, he reminded me of Frank Schmitt, my department chair at MIT. The philanthropist Laurence Rockefeller was devoted to the Sloan-Kettering Institute (SKI). He became a frequent visitor, exhibiting sincere interest and pride in what we were doing. He and Rhoads promoted a close sense of shared mission among researchers at every level. As a new "Dr.," I relished the privilege of lunching in the "Doctors' Dining Room." There, whether junior or senior in status, we talked together about science and medicine—and politics! My original operating assumption—that my colleagues were all wiser than I was—was challenged in conversation about the new, soon-to-be infamous, Kinsey report on *Sexual Behavior of the Human Male.* I laughed (to myself) when one distinguished physician said, seriously, referring to the high-income New Jersey suburb in which he lived, "I don't think they interviewed in Upper Montclair!"

An early family portrait, 1956

Electron microscopy was then in its infancy. Virtually everything we viewed in this machine was visible at a higher magnification than previously possible. It is hard to describe the daily thrill of seeing some of nature's microscopic architecture for the first time. The few biologists then using electron microscopes in the U.S., U.K. and Europe readily consulted with each other, visiting each other's labs. Keith Porter and George Palade, leaders in these new approaches to cell structure, were kind and generous colleagues who often invited me to visit and consult with them in their Rockefeller laboratories across the street.

As I began using SKI's microscope, my thoughts turned back to the clam muscle and my Ph.D. research. Now I could see, rather than just imagine, the submicroscopic structure of its fibers and membranes. During a Woods Hole summer, I collected and examined muscle samples from many animal species, including jellyfish. Specimens for electron microscope examination must be chemically "fixed" to prevent deterioration during examination. Structures were distinguished by applying chemical stains that various molecules absorb differently. After being fixed and stained, specimens had to be sliced as thinly and evenly as possible to maximize the clarity of the image projected on a photographic or fluorescent screen. Specimens were then placed on a glass slide and positioned within the interior vacuum of the electron microscope. In those days, the entire machine was, roughly, double the size of an old-fashioned upright piano, and enclosed in a light-and-temperature controlled room. In this machine, I could actually *see*, for the first time that all the muscles were made up of smaller fibers, invisible under the light microscope. Calling these "myofibrils" ("myo" for muscle), I was now seeing with my own eyes the cellular structures whose molecular alignment I had only imagined at MIT.

Although my tool had changed, my research question remained the same: "What unknown structures can this tool help me reveal within biological cells? Sitting in a dark room, peering at an image on a fluorescent screen while manipulating the machine's controls to view the image is much like viewing a TV show, albeit on a much smaller screen. Scanning electron microscope images is like surfing the Internet. For a biologist, viewing a TV show cannot compare with viewing the previously unseen secrets of cancer cells! Day after day, hours at a time, and throughout three pregnancies, I took photographs of biological structures never before visible at such high magnification. Nature wrote the scripts for these visual stories, not a TV studio or novelist. Our job was to write the story that would fit the previously unseen realities we were viewing. Nature builds structures with form, balance, rhythm and symmetry that the human eye and brain register aesthetically as beauty . . . and that attract our attention and curiosity. How satisfying it was, intellectually and artistically, for us human beings to see more and more of these intriguing and attractive structures!

Electron microscopes operate on the same principle as light microscopes, using electromagnetic lenses instead of glass lenses to focus electrons, rather than light beams, on the specimens. The images are recorded on photographic film or a fluorescent screen. The quality of the resultant images varies depending upon how thinly and evenly each specimen is sliced. The day we learned that the sharp edge of plate glass is sharper than any knife, and we found ways to make glass knives from broken edges of glass, we were as excited as if we had just landed on a new planet to explore it for the first time! Needing soft tissue with which to test the glass knives, I asked Charlotte Friend for a specimen from the cancerous mice she was working with. She and I had started working for Alice Moore on the same day in 1949: Charlotte with her brand new Ph.D. in microbiology from Yale University and me finishing up mine in physical biology at MIT. Charlotte was a born-and-bred New Yorker, a graduate of Hunter High School and Hunter College before attending Yale. We became fast friends and lunched together almost daily. Examining the cells within the specimen Charlotte had given me, I saw some small hexagonally close-packed particles and excitedly asked Charlotte to take a look. I had not seen this similarity in other cells, nor had anyone reported such findings. Here was an "oddity," an anomaly that Charlotte and I started exploring together. Charlotte's work included injecting mice with various potions prepared by Alice Moore as part of her search for cancer-killing viruses. She worked with live animals, cells and viruses while I worked with the clean inanimate tools of electron microscopes and glass knives. Showing Charlotte the images I had photographed, I said, "Whatever these things are, they must all be the same size." MIT's crystallography courses had taught me that round bodies of the same size pack together in hexagonal patterns. This was important, because the bodies in my images were being sliced in different ways and in different directions, so did not always look alike, but their hexagonal close packing was unmistakable.

Our work together was governed by questions like "What are the particles in this photograph?" and "Do they relate to cancer?" Our first hypothesis was that they were viruses. No electron microscope images of viruses had yet been published, but my images were the right size to be viruses, yet too small to be bacteria. The tobacco mosaic virus was known to aggregate in a crystalline pattern. That other viruses would also aggregate closely enough to form crystals was not surprising. With my electron micrographs and her mouse data, we had enough evidence to suggest, in the paper we published, that we had observed "virus-like" particles in certain mouse cells.

This story illustrates the characteristics of good research: educated curiosity, collaboration and good luck. Charlotte and I worked happily together, bringing different strengths to our work. It was our good fortune that the virus particles were present and even visible in the particular slices I observed. As a skilled microbiologist, Charlotte kept records that enabled her to identify the mouse from which my specimen came, and then develop the mouse from which this specimen came into a strain of mice from which she identified a mouse leukemic virus that became known as the Friend Virus.

During this period at Sloan-Kettering, my horizons were stretched in multiple ways, within my research work and beyond. James Hillier, then director of RCA's famous Sarnoff Research Laboratory, was my first contact with an industrial scientist. He had earned his Ph.D. at the University of Toronto in 1946 for the design of an electron microscope, a microscope then commercially developed by RCA. As the director of RCA's research labs, he was eager to explore biological applications for this microscopy, and decided to try to send electron micrograph images through television screens. Using our facilities for this work, he became a regular visitor to my lab.

Other scientists at the Institute were interested in our work and would bring me questions to suggest for electron microscopic study. In 1956, two well-known skin pathologists at Memorial Hospital (a husband and wife team) persuaded me to look at the structure of the top layer of the skin, the epidermis. Since I needed specimens that were soft to cut, they suggested tissue from babies' circumcisions. Using my glass knives to prepare super-thin sections of this tissue, we got some stunning images. I published highly magnified pictures of these skin cells, comparing them visually with the same tissue at lower magnification. The viewer could then identify, at low magnification, the site in the tissues that the high magnification images reflected. Our pictures contributed new information about the bridges between cells in the upper layer of skin and cells in the underlying connective tissue. This was tremendously satisfying research. I still enjoy looking back at the images we obtained, and even today I learn, through a scientific database, that my papers are downloaded by someone, somewhere in the world each week. Scientific research can provide intellectual immortality!

Curious about my work, Don Fawcett, head of the Department of Anatomy at Cornell Medical College across the street, came to visit my lab. Discussing my interest in cancer cells, he rightly said, "If you want to learn about structures in cancer cells, perhaps you should learn more about structures inside normal cells." He added, "The best way for you to learn cytology (cell structure) would be to teach it. Why don't you come across the street to work with me and to teach histology to medical students?" Working with an expert electron microscopist and biologist seemed like a great opportunity. For the next three years, Don Fawcett and I studied the same intercellular bridges I had first photographed at SKI in skin tissue, but now in a different tissue—the heart muscle. We published several papers illuminating important details in the bridges we found between cells in this muscle. To support this research, I was appointed as Instructor in Histology (the cellular organization of organs) for first-year medical students at Cornell Medical College (now Weill Cornell Medical College). As an Instructor, my job was to wander through the immense laboratory where students were working, answer their questions and help them use their microscopes. Presenting class lectures on muscle and skin was also among my assignments. Thus, my first teaching experience was with medical students.

An accomplished photographer with an excellent eye for design and form, Fawcett spent hours in the darkroom, orienting and printing electron micrographs himself, rather than leaving this work to a technician. His scientific publications became known for the "beauty" of his micrographs, a beauty that attracted and engaged the viewer. I tried for the same effect in mine, was happy when one of my micrographs remained for years as an illustration in a popular textbook (*A Textbook of Histology* by Alexander A. Maximow and William Bloom). Another one of my electron micrographs was published in a modest little book called *Powers of Ten* that illustrated the level of magnification available through high powered microscopy.

Working at the medical school, I missed Charlotte Friend. She went on to a successful career as a cancer virologist, well respected worldwide for identifying viruses. Through her work on carcinogenic viruses, she was fulfilling her lifelong passion: to help cure disease. Also devoted to advancing women in science, she became the first female president of the New York Academy of Sciences. Charlotte never married—her work was her passion. I relish memories of our days together: fun and laughter, talking about ideas and observations we made or read about, and sharing decisions and counsel as I explored my own decisions about marriage and life. While I was busy dating and wondering who I was going to marry, Charlotte devotedly cared for her mother and her science. She was tremendously gratified by her work. . . except when she found it "not nice." In my last visit with Charlotte in her lab in the late 1980s, she said to me, "Science is not as nice as it used to be." She was referring to increasing competition and emerging politics entering the scientific community. There are no rules for the happiness and success of any of us, let alone for women in science.

In those days, there were no policies about maternity leave, so I simply took time off without pay, to stay at home for six weeks or more with each new baby. I also arranged to spend the summer months by the seaside with my little boys. Sometimes I was able to combine this time with writing articles reporting on my work. At other times, I worked four days a week. With all the time I took off post-babies and in the summer, I assumed that these generous personnel policies were possible because no one else was competing for my job, and my status was still that of a junior researcher. No one else at SKI was doing electron microscopy, so I was not competing for advancement. My research superiors wrote the funding proposals, while I wrote the detailed scientific articles reporting my findings. Comparing my experiences as a young scientist with those of other women at that time, I realized how fortunate I was to be working with scientists who were genuinely gender-blind. Thanks to Dusty Rhoads' leadership, Sloan-Kettering was notable for the diversity of its scientists. He hired significant women scientists in the early years. Alice Moore's small department was majority female. At Sloan-Kettering, as a continually pregnant scientist, I was a minority of one. In my teaching at Cornell Medical College, I was the only female faculty in histology, only a couple of years older than my students, the only female in the classroom or lab and surely the only woman with three small boys at home.

In those days, all the medical students were male, and were eager to ask me questions about their wives' reproductive tracts. One of my students, now a prominent New York ophthalmologist, recognized my name when I came to see him as a patient. He well remembers my talking about "birefringence" in the light in his microscope—and also of my witty response to a student, full of innuendo, who tried involving me in a sexual joke. According to him, I made a remark that put him in his place. I do not recall this, but it suggests that there was more sexual harassment going on than I bothered to remember.

When I was pregnant with my son Bill, I was invited to attend a major conference in Houston, Texas, to report on my studies of skin. When I asked a successful woman M.D. at the hospital whether at eight months pregnant I ought to go, her response was, "Of course you should go. Would you want anyone else to be identified with your discoveries?" I listened. I went. I had a great time. In their coverage of the conference, the *Houston Post* printed a photo of me, unmistakably pregnant—an unusual newspaper image in those days!

This was a romantic time for my field of cell biology and for my husband's field of medicine. Both areas were starting new growth cycles, born of new discoveries fed by new technologies. My husband was not jealous of my work. He said, "It would be great if you won the Nobel Prize. I would not have to work so hard." After presenting my maiden talk in Sloan-Kettering's largest auditorium, I found him accepting congratulations as the audience filed out in the back of the hall, while I was greeting those in the front. In my field of cell biology, new tools were advancing our ability to learn more and more about biological structures. As other new tools were designed and manufactured, biology became physical biology, then molecular biology, and now systems biology and mathematical biology, which often circles back to organismic biology. Modern applied physics, triumphant during World War II, first led this growth. During the 1950s, research funding was plentiful. Electron microscopy was a novel, pioneering technique, attracting lots of financial support. Public perceptions of science were not yet a concern. Scientists felt that the public loved us. Science and technology had helped win the war, so popular support for scientific research became a post-war fallout of this achievement. My researcher's salary, drawn from both Sloan-Kettering and Cornell, was supported by government as well as private philanthropy funding. For me, it was a great time to be doing science. I did learn from friends that sexism was alive and well in other scientific workplaces, so I continued to try to do my job in a way that would keep the door open for other women to follow.

Our laboratory attracted visits from distinguished cell biologists from abroad, particularly those from Scandinavia and elsewhere in Europe. Often from privileged educational and aristocratic backgrounds, their charm and style added to our lab environment. Just as in Woods Hole, I observed that scientists, like all professionals, come in diverse tastes, styles and interests. George Palade of Rockefeller University was a friendly, gracious, elegant Rumanian émigré who later earned the Nobel Prize for his work. During one of my visits to his lab, we were discussing how to name some structures his group had just discovered within the large bodies inside cells called mitochondria. Calling upon his classical education, Palade offered, "Cristae mitochondriales." His familiarity with the classics and with the European authors he could quote was impressive—and not common among my U.S. colleagues. For a brief period I shared a lab with Chester Southam, a physician particularly emotionally devoted to curing disease. Both Chet and his wife had contracted tuberculosis through their work in clinics. I remember him telling me fondly of the prisoners who volunteered to participate in his research. Like other physician colleagues, he was determined that I, exploring cancer only microscopically, should know something about the macro world of cancer patients. Inviting me to join him on medical rounds, I met a patient I will never forget: a young mother fatally ill with metastatic melanoma. Thus began my lifelong fear of melanoma, and my sympathy for those suffering from it. My visits to Porter and Palade, or other colleagues at Rockefeller University, were always a treat. Often they included invitations to play tennis on their lovely courts, now torn up to make room for new laboratories. Dining in their wood-paneled dining room overlooking the East River, I felt proud to be a member of an honored tribe.

What did "science" mean to me then? Every day, I went to work believing that what I was doing would help medicine, help people and help cure cancer. It continued to be my way of thanking the world for my education and other privileges. Beyond personal intellectual exhilaration, there was the thrill of being part of a private world of professionals—male and female, U.S. and international—all of whom liked to solve problems through scientific modes of inquiry. Although not sharing a special vocabulary that served all of our disciplines, we did share the philosophy and mode of inquiry. Before building and economic issues closed the Doctors' Dining Room at Sloan-Kettering, I was grateful for the opportunity it gave me, a young Ph.D., to listen to mature scientists and physicians in luncheon conversations. . . and even to join in.

At the Rockefeller Institute, the dining room was elegant with its wood paneling, table service and a magnificent view of the East River. Around its tables, conversation about work focused on the questions being asked, experiments being done and patient diagnoses made. My colleagues had great questions: why did you ask this question rather than another? How did you design your experiment? Why did you choose to do it this way? What is the evidence for your diagnosis? What do you hope to find? These questions that govern scientific inquiry are open to anyone. Scientists challenge each other on claims made for evidence, on how and why the inquiry was undertaken. In this way, I learned that the scientific literacy scientists and engineers share is our understanding and use of scientific inquiry, the mode of problem-solving we all use. This helped me understand that I belonged to a scientifically, medically and technologically literate club, an international club whose members shared education, behavior and values about science—and all intellectual problem solving.

Although I was happy and productive "at the bench" in laboratories, and suffered no sexist obstacles at home or at work, conflicts between my marriage, children and job eventually led me to leave research. My youngest son, Russell, was two years old and I had increased housekeeping responsibilities as we had moved to a narrow four-story brownstone house on East 87th Street, close to a park and the East River. When I decided to give up research and stay home with my children, my reasons were specific to my family situation and personal needs. Others might have resolved the same issues differently. It was not obstacles at work, but my personal beliefs about bringing up boys that prompted my departure from Cornell. These beliefs sound old-fashioned, even sexist, today, so perhaps *I* was sexist! I thought that boys, in particular, should not have an "all-knowing mother," that I should never say to them, "Don't bother mother, she's thinking." Yes, doing good science requires lots and lots of "thinking time"—usually more than "doing time," and bringing up children requires lots of "being together" time as well. With every day, I was discovering what excellent company they were!

In writing about conflicts between time on the job and time at home, a 1950s Radcliffe College report on graduate education for women noted, "It still takes an afternoon to spend an afternoon with a child." I decided to keep company with my children, rather than dreaming up good ideas about intercellular bridges. Where did I get this idea? Perhaps from relationships I observed between children and their scientist mothers in Woods Hole, and from popular psychology about mothers and sons. I felt thoroughly spoiled by working with brilliant and creative scientists and knew well the kind of inspiration and devotion that made their work great. To analyze cell structures creatively, I knew I should wake up at night thinking about them—twisting them around in my mind, as Jim Watson had said he did with the DNA helix. To fulfill my love and responsibility for my family, on the other hand, I believed that I should instead wake up worrying about chicken pox, ways to entertain to support my husband's medical practice. With all I have learned since then, I am sorry that I did not involve my sons more closely with the ideas and problem-solving I loved. Recognizing that I was fortunate in being able to put the best interests of my family first, I made my decision to leave and did not look back.

5

GIRLS' SCHOOLING AND SCOUTING

Science promotes critical inquiry, curiosity and democracy.
Through its focus on evidence and honesty, science provides
a way to call the bluff of those who would lie to us.
                    —RAMPELE MANPHELA, VICE-CHANCELLOR,
                    UNIVERSITY OF CAPE TOWN, 1999

IN 1956, RADCLIFFE'S PRESIDENT, Wilbur K. Jordan, invited me to address the college's graduating class. Now a ten-year alumna, I was flattered with the invitation and assumed that he saw me as an alumna on a fast track, with children and a significant job, and thought I would provide the graduating class an uplifting pro-career message, which I tried to do. I began by saying that managing jobs and careers would be no problem for Radcliffe graduates, but managing housekeeping probably would. I suggested that family-friendly work can well be found in not-for-profit organizations, and added that, although they are less financially rewarding, they are likely to provide the flexibility and work schedule that mixing family and work responsibilities requires. I also recommended this approach because it is societally important work that many husbands believe they cannot afford to take. From the look on the president's face, I realized these remarks surprised him. My point of view may be considered sexist and "old-fashioned" today, but it felt right at the time. Speaking to the audience that day, little did I foresee that only three years later I would be following my own advice and moving from competitive full-time research to teaching school—or that Radcliffe's appointment office would help make this happen!

My invitation to address Radcliffe seniors had not come out of the blue. In the late 1950s, I was asked to help Radcliffe's admissions office by interviewing New York candidates for admission. As I talked with these applicants in my living room, I found myself asking the questions Dean Cronkhite had asked me more than ten years before: "Why do you want to come to this college?" "What do you enjoy most at school?" "What books are you reading?" And, if they were suburban girls, I asked, "What do you do in your trips to New York City?" Some girls answered the "Why?" question by telling me that they wanted a college education to make sure they could take care of their families if something happened to their husbands. This answer surprised me and piqued my curiosity about the education of girls: a topic that kept me busy for years to come.

A telephone call from Radcliffe's appointment office informed me that "a small independent girl's school in New York is looking for a high school science teacher. All the science classes are scheduled in the morning, so you could have the afternoon free to be with your children." The caller then asked, "Would you be interested?" I loved my sons' company and was trying to manage at home without the extra domestic help I had had when working full-time. But, with boys running up and down three flights of stairs in our narrow home, a household to manage and a social life to promote for my husband's new radiology practice, I soon yearned for more help at home—and more professional contact outside. Before I heard from Radcliffe about this opportunity, I had sought advice from a woman who had successfully "done it all." Millicent McIntosh was a neighbor and considered an icon for all of us young career-minded New York women. She had been headmistress of the Brearley School, an eminent K–12 independent school, and was now president of Barnard College. With her husband and children, she lived in a townhouse almost adjacent to ours on East 87th Street. I explained to her that I was looking for work that would be compatible with bringing up children and asked whether there might be a job for me at Barnard College. She then offered some direct and practical advice: "At Barnard, faculty and staff meetings start at 4:00 p.m. and run until at least 6:00 p.m., just when you will want to be home with your children. Why don't you look into independent schools? That is the only work I know that would enable you and your children to have the same working hours and holidays."

Based on my conversation with Millicent and this admissions experience in mind, it did not take me long to tell the Radcliffe Appointment Office that I would be interested in the part-time science teaching job they mentioned. It could pay for a full-time nanny at home, and I welcomed the chance to continue with science. The Lenox School (today the co-ed Birch Wathen Lenox School) was a small school for girls from first to twelfth grades situated on a tree-lined street of elegant residences on Manhattan's Upper East Side. Initially it was a "finishing school," like most private girls' schools, but by the mid-1900s it was academically competitive with schools for boys. Its founder, Jessica Cosgrave, was forceful and outspoken in her crusade for women's rights, combining career, marriage and motherhood in her own life. She founded Finch Junior College and then Lenox School in 1916. Olivia Green became headmistress in 1929 and led the school through the Depression and other crises. By 1958, she was determined to strengthen Lenox's science offerings, so she renovated a small room in the basement for a laboratory and set about searching for an instructor—who turned out to be me. I interviewed for the teaching job and was impressed by her determination and flexibility, and liked the schedule she offered. Happily, I accepted.

Teaching earth science, biology and chemistry required my boning up on high school texts. Earth science was a particular problem because I had never studied geology and knew nothing about rocks. In reviewing some textbooks, I was in for some distressing surprises. I learned that pupils had to memorize names like "sedimentary" and "metamorphic" without spending time on what the words meant. Since my own science classes had not stayed in my memory, I felt free to determine how I thought the subject should be taught. A lifelong lesson about good teaching came when a student asked a particularly challenging question, one for which I did not have an easy response. Instead of giving her a superficial answer, I decided to treat her question as we would in graduate school, replying, "I don't know the answer, so let's try to find it together." Then followed a good class discussion and a lifelong friendship with this student, Elizabeth Reed. Years later she told me that I was the first teacher who had ever told her, "I don't know." "And," she added, "one with a Ph.D." I guess this class was a success!

Headmistress at her desk, Lenox School, 1960s

It was a complete surprise when, during my year of teaching, Miss Green decided to retire as headmistress, and the school's board of trustees offered me her job. An alumna later told me that Miss Green spoke of her delight in finding someone young and scientifically inclined to take over the school. Indeed, now I recognized her strategy in bringing me to the school. In considering her offer, I consulted Jim Hubbell, headmaster of my sons' school. He said, "As a headmaster, I find that everything I have ever studied and everything I do contributes to my job. Attending a concert, reading a book and playing with my own children all help build the skills, values and information I need as a headmaster." That sounded good to me. Together with the advice from Millicent McIntosh and Miss Green's confidence in me, I decided to accept the job offer. My husband said that although he was "not interested in other people's children," he was happy with my working at a school and very much welcomed the additional income. So at 32 years old, I set off on a new and entirely unforeseen career path.

The Lenox job changed much in our lives, including our morning routine. Five of us left the house and piled into our car together. We first dropped off one boy at preschool, two at The Buckley School, and me at my school. My husband then left himself and the car at his hospital. When schedules permitted, I would pick up some of the boys at the end of the day. In later years, when they could travel independently, they would sometimes pick me up before going home. At home, a delightful young German woman whom I selected as nanny was teaching us the song, "Que sera, sera . . .whatever will be, will be. The future's not ours to see." These words came back to me again and again as I lived through all the changes and challenges of my early years of marriage and motherhood.

Norman, Bill and Russell spent all of their pre-high school years at The Buckley School, four short blocks along Lexington Avenue from Lenox. As I could readily walk from my school to theirs to attend their class performances or exhibits, I became a very familiar presence at Buckley. Perhaps my most vivid memory of our shared school years came on the day President John F. Kennedy was killed. As soon as I heard the news, determined to share it with my sons, I left Lenox and headed to the music school across from Buckley where Bill was having a violin lesson and then crossed the street with him to collect his brothers so we could all go home and talk and watch the news together. Another vivid memory includes an energy blackout in New York that left our neighborhood in total darkness. The two younger boys got home before dark, but Norman took the wrong bus and had a very long walk home in the blackout. He finally made it, finding us all anxiously waiting with candles lit.

With us all only a few short blocks apart, I asked my staff to support my wish that the boys be allowed to come directly into my office whenever they called for me. I believed they should feel at home in my workplace and not be expected to knock. Sometimes a Lenox parent was surprised to have a conference with her daughter's headmistress interrupted by a young boy—even one young enough to climb onto his mother's lap. While my eldest son Norman was still in school, I asked how he felt about growing up with a working mother. His answer was immediate and brief: "It was great. We could use your gym, your library and the school station wagon—and have birthday parties in your dining room." Trust children to clearly recognize their material benefits! These were very happy years for me, sharing school and home with my sons. I was pursuing my own learning about teaching in my school, while my boys were engaged in their own learning in theirs. Life was so busy and the problems I was trying to solve were so interesting that, although I looked back fondly to my science, there was no time to miss it.

I soon discovered that my faculty viewed science as "for experts only," and the experts did not include themselves or their students. Science was perceived as abstruse, and culturally divorced from the arts and humanities—in other words, not appropriate for preparing Lenox's privileged girls for their futures. I became as passionate about access to science for all girls as I had been about access for myself. My first step in this direction was to engage an able and lively Williams College graduate as a science teacher, and to plot and plan with her to dispel the myth that science in school is "for nerds only." We initiated a primary- and middle-school science program emphasizing student-made projects, which we then displayed in our well-traveled corridors. Models of biological cells, crystal structures, volcanoes and the Milky Way appeared on the walls and in the corridors, eventually becoming as well displayed as student artwork. As the non-science teachers grew interested in these displays, and asked questions about them, slowly but surely attitudes started to change. More and more, teachers, students and parents became curious, asking questions and studying the displays, and became interested in the classes themselves. As more science was included in the curriculum, lower and middle school teachers asked for access to a science specialist to enrich their teaching. For high school courses we included a variety of field trips and also some of the innovative curricula being developed in the 1960s. By the time I left the school in 1972, many Lenox graduates were choosing, as Elizabeth had, to major in the sciences in college. Whereas once I had been the only science teacher at Lenox, by the time I left, thirteen years later, science courses (as well as cross-cultural courses like anthropology and psychology) were taught throughout the school.

Although I was no longer working as a "scientist," I could not stop thinking like one! I approached problems in the analytical ways with which I was familiar: framing questions and working out their solutions. Accustomed as I was to framing hypotheses, I would try various guesses about what the answer should be, until I found one that worked.

One good example of this problem solving was the way we addressed students' geometry problems. At Lenox, as in most schools, geometry was offered in tenth grade. Noticing that some students had consistent difficulty with this subject, I started asking why. Was the student lazy, or the teacher poor? Was there a home problem, or an innate inability? Knowing both the teacher and the students well, I could eliminate all possible guesses for answers (hypotheses) except one: ability. What skill is used in geometry more than in other subjects? Poor visual skills became a hypothesis. The ability to "see" and remember a triangle, its sides and its angles in one's mind's "eye" is essential to geometrical proofs. Where else in school does visual memory particularly help? For me, my good visual memory helped in memorizing vocabulary lists in French and Latin. When I learned that students who did poorly in geometry also had trouble with languages, I reviewed the scores on a cognitive test (Stanford-Binet) we gave all students. We soon discovered that poor geometry students tested low in visual memory. Bingo! With the visual hypothesis thus confirmed, we decided to meld geometry and algebra curricula in grades nine and ten to enable those with less keen visual memory to balance their difficulties in geometry with success in algebra, less dependent on visualization. We also alerted language teachers to the influence of visual memory in working with vocabulary lists. The outcome? Students did not feel "stupid" because they had trouble in geometry—or languages. We helped them understand that, although their visual memory might not be as keen as that of some others, they had other cognitive skills and senses with which to compensate.

Happily, I found that the management and the hands-on skills necessary to design and conduct science experiments were transferable to many of my new tasks: getting a boiler fixed, raising money, designing curricula, hiring teachers and organizing public relations. I sought answers to the questions inherent in these diverse tasks in much the same way: finding the most appropriate question to ask and then testing guesses (hypotheses) to find the most helpful answer. The collaborative habits I was accustomed to in academe also helped facilitate relationships with trustees, parents, faculty and staff. I soon developed the golden rule that when a team is doing very well one year, adding a new assignment or a new person helps keep momentum going—just as we would add another variable to a science experiment. Adding energy combats the tendency of moving bodies to slow down in life, just as in physics!

I soon learned, however, that teaching and learning involves so many variables that the single answers available through scientific inquiry are rare indeed. With only one class at each grade level, I could observe teaching strategies in our classes easily and informally. I asked our much-admired first-grade teacher, Doris Weeks, about how the brain learns: how it relates images (letters) to sound (words), and to meaning. Her reply—"Nothing that I know of"—taught me that what this teacher "knew" came from her decades of teaching experience, her trying and evaluating the various aural, visual, tactile, aesthetic and intellectual strategies best adapted to each student's learning styles and needs. Her effectiveness came not from any single method or research data, but from what her experience had taught her was the best strategy for each child. Trying to explain her teaching strategy to me, she said, "With a new pupil, the first thing I do is engage her personally with me, and then [gesturing] turn the student's attention away from me to a book." Thus, I learned from Mrs. Weeks that school teaching begins with a personal relationship. When a mother told me that her daughter had described middle-aged, bespectacled Mrs. Weeks as "beautiful," I understood that a young child might consider "beautiful" as a way to describe someone valuable to her. Year after year, I watched first-graders leave happy after their first day at school as they brought home something they had made or read—a new book or perhaps a drawing—and they stayed happy and engaged with their learning with Mrs. Weeks all year.

My school management skills were also improved by all my housekeeping at home. At professional meetings with school heads, many headmasters noted that operating with continuing deficits did help prod their schools' fundraising. I preferred a more direct approach and managed to keep the school within budget, just as I did our household expenses. Our parents association helped with fundraising while the alumnae and I started an alumnae association that set up procedures to track and keep in touch with Lenox graduates. By 1968, I was reporting to the board on alumnae activities and beginning to form development and endowment funds.

That I was the only headmistress in New York City who had children of her own did not escape the attention of the local independent school newsletter:[1].

> *Mrs. Selby is a striking example of the educated woman of today who has combined happily a variety of roles. She attributes this to having studied in depth at an early age, to having pursued advanced academic training in fields where many men cannot afford to work and where a crying need exists for trained minds. Women, she feels, have an obligation to enter those fields where they can complement rather than compete with men. Especially in research work and in secondary schools, they are needed. Women in these fields have freedom and flexibility, for they do not demand a nine-to-five day or a twelve-month year. Thus, the educated woman can achieve freedom for professional pursuits without having to deny any of her feminine drives and responsibilities or effectiveness as a woman.*

I was still promoting the ideas and the fantasies that characterized my 1956 talk to Radcliffe graduates.

The educational approaches we introduced in the 1960s reflected real-world connections and the self-expression of those years. On my tenth anniversary as headmistress, the school had an abundance of applicants, and could boast of individualized teaching, study carrels, elective courses, field trips and discussion groups. When an alumna told me, recently, that she felt she had attended a "progressive" school, I remembered how I used to answer people who asked about Lenox's teaching philosophy: "We cultivate the garden, but also feed the flowers." One more lasting influence of my ninth grade at the Dalton School.

One of the school's objectives was not so easily achieved: diversification of the student body. We admitted several daughters of Muslim members of United Nation delegations, and I also enrolled a close relative of the Dalai Lama—until she discovered she was pregnant. A male colleague at the Collegiate School and I had heard of "A Better Chance" (the "ABC Program"), which promoted access to academic

---

1. The newsletter was the *Parents League Bulletin*; quote estimated to be from 1962.

private boarding schools for gifted underprivileged graduates of public junior high schools. Saying to each other, "Why not day schools?" we developed a strong relationship with Eduard Plummer, a guidance counselor at Wadleigh Junior High School in Harlem. Plummer devised an academic boot camp, preparing boys and girls for the secondary school test and offering etiquette classes. Characteristically, he said to his students, "There will be those who don't want you there, but you have to go. You are the Jackie Robinson of education. If he could do what he did, you can open the doors to those who will follow behind you."

Plummer introduced us to minority students who could cope well with our curriculum and also with breaking social barriers by coming to a private school outside their immediate neighborhood. We invited other independent schools to join us and launched the "New York Independent School Opportunity Project." When interviewing the mother of a girl who became one of the first of these students to attend Lenox, I asked if there was a quiet place at home where the girl could study. When she told me that she had already picked out the spot in their apartment and bought a desk for her daughter, I accepted her right away. Thereafter, Mrs. McCoy became a familiar person at school events. Her daughter, Diane, graduated from Lenox successfully and happily, and later became a dean at Columbia University. Diane certainly put into practice Plummer's mandate in terms of opening doors for those who will follow you. Other fine young women did follow her, as I found ways to pay their tuition from the school's operating budget.

Slowly but surely, I decided that most challenges of the 1960s were born of questioning the attitude that "Father Knows Best." One example of questioning "father" came when students tested the structure of traditional student governments. Lenox, like most schools, had a hierarchical student government, in which classes elected their presidents, and then class presidents elected the school's student president. But one day a senior student asked for an appointment with me to ask why one student alone should represent her class. Shouldn't each individual also have the chance to have her opinions heard? Again, a great "new" question, and again, I suggested we find the answer together. Following discussions school-wide, the students created, and faculty supported, a town meeting structure for student government. Our small size made this manageable. Only later did I learn, while attending a national meeting of independent school heads, that other independent schools were also making the transition from a representational hierarchy to a town meeting. Without Facebook, Twitter or any other social organizing medium, students in different parts of the country were urging their schools to change at the same time, and in the same way.

In another sign of the times in the late 60s, we made gym and other activities optional to allow senior students to engage in neighborhood community/political activities. Again, no parents—or trustees—objected. But, I am ashamed to recall my response the first time a student came to talk to me about her concerns over the Vietnam War. All I could think of saying was to suggest she write her congressman. Shortly thereafter I invited speakers knowledgeable about the war and related matters to address the student body. Again, we decided to undertake the inquiry *with the students* rather than as "experts" preaching from above.

Feminism came to Lenox through speakers like Bella Abzug and Columbia's Catharine Stimpson. When my neighbor, Millicent McIntosh, accepted an invitation to speak, I relished how, in her remarks, she noted to the students that I was "bringing my children up on the street," just as she had, and by "the street" she meant 87th Street, where her children had played, and where mine were now. I thought of that presentation again when I was in the audience for her last formal address to Barnard College on the occasion of her retirement. I agreed with her remarks that the professional advancement of women depended on the availability and quality of domestic help. Margaret Mead spoke to us about the changing attitudes then underway, paying particular attention to attitudes toward marriage. My memories of those days are of all of us—parents, students and teachers—learning together about what the term "feminism" meant, and what it should mean for each of us personally and globally.

I addressed such issues directly with students and faculty at Monday morning assemblies. Before my remarks, we sang hymns like "For the Beauty of the Earth" and "For Those in Peril on the Sea," just as we had in my English and Canadian schools. Moving from the sublime to the relevant, I would try to speak about issues of the day. Most Sundays evenings at home were spent thinking up and writing these remarks. And, yes, it was the 60s of "sex, drugs and rock and roll," so sex education and drug education came to Lenox School too. As societal problems with drug use mounted, I finally screwed up the courage to speak about them one morning in November 1969. Part of what I said was:

> *I have not spoken to you, formally, from my position here about drugs before because I frankly have felt inadequate to the task. Having no personal experience with drugs at your age, or any age, I have felt humbled by the enormity of the temptations of the drug world that surround you. The temptations of possible shortcuts to experience, to creativity, to courage, to poise, to self-confidence are tragically more compelling at your age before you have achieved these goals the lasting way, through living . . . . But how can we over-35-year-olders, who can't be trusted anyway, tell you it is worth waiting for the ecstasy, the joys, the inspirations, the ups and downs, that your God-given body and your love of others will bring you?*

As a postscript to my talk, I spoke to the students about attending a lecture by Timothy Leary, famous for his recommendations of LSD. I told students that I recognized that the large photographs he displayed, presumably of LSD "highs," were taken with what we then called "phase contrast" microscopy. Thus, I could relate my aesthetic pleasures in looking through microscopes to Leary's accounts of his LSD highs! I also told them that after hearing Leary's talk, I felt proud and happy with life as I was living it with my undrugged mind and body—and hoped that they would too.

We did have a couple of drug issues with cases of students using painkillers they found in their parents' medicine cabinets. Only one problem led to suspending an eighth grade student from school. She did not respond to counseling, leaving us convinced that she would continue to set a bad example for her classmates. Years later, the girl's mother and I became good colleagues. I then learned of her suffering from unrelenting lifelong behavioral problems. While reassured that I had made the right decision for Lenox when the girl was a student, I was saddened to learn of her continuing difficulties and proud of my continuing friendship with her parents.

By 1969, we were offering an integrated sequence of sex education from grades six through twelve. Parents who did not wish their daughters to participate or had questions were urged to speak to me; no one did. Students were also supportive. Once, when I was moderating a workshop on Sex and Religion, a meeting of students from all New York independent schools, I started to summarize what we had talked about. A couple of girls spoke up, almost in unison: "Mrs. Selby, please don't summarize. We want to go home to think about what we talked about today, and draw our own conclusions." Herewith was another lasting lesson in teaching and learning.

Maintaining good relations with students' families was part of my daily life, while professional meetings of independent school administrators and teachers provided long-term learning and friendships. At a meeting of the New York State Association of Independent Schools, I took a step toward leadership among peers. Together with several male school heads, I was working to promote some new legislation in Albany. While we were meeting, they identified three or four of us to form a group to meet legislators. Surprised that no one brought up my name, I spoke up: "You know, that is something I would like to do." Immediately the answer was, "Great, Cecily. So glad you can do it—you must join us." It was then that I discovered that there are moments when, despite what the older girls at Wycombe Abbey had said, it is okay to be bumptious—albeit polite and gracious at the same time! With that experience I continued to speak up, when I wanted to, among my peers. However, my ambition to keep the door open for women who would follow often led me to a generally laid-back approach.

A couple of years before I left Lenox I was elected to the presidency of an organization called the Headmistresses of the East and was able to joke that I was "President of the Chief Concubines of the East." This distinguished group still goes by the same name, continuing to foster collegiality, support and inspiration for today's heads of girls' schools. All independent schools were grappling with "Father Knows Best" challenges, student unrest, and drug use. After they left Buckley, my sons and their friends suffered considerably from prep school leadership that placed institutional needs ahead of those of students. The best word on this subject came at a professional meeting of heads of private schools. Following a discussion of when and when not to expel a student, an experienced headmaster said, "The sink-or-swim philosophy is very hard on human souls." That warning became one of my mantras for all my educational work that followed.

Headmistresses in those days rarely left their schools for other jobs. When I left the school to lead a much larger community of girls and women, Girl Scouts of the U.S.A., the students acknowledged this development by writing in their yearbook, "We have been fortunate to be led by a woman who put no limits on her own ambition." A Lenox graduate once told me, "You encouraged us girls to reach for the skies."

Once again, it was an unexpected phone call—this time, combined with a son's advice—that sent me off in a new direction. It was 1971 and I had just come home from a day at Lenox. My son Norman was home from college, sitting in the kitchen with me as I prepared dinner. Chatting with him about my day, I mentioned that an executive recruiter had phoned to ask whether I would consider becoming a candidate for a position as National Executive Director of the Girl Scouts of the U.S.A. When Norman asked how I replied, I said my answer was "No, thanks." Norman replied, "Why not, Ma? If you really care about all those socio-economic issues you're always talking about, that is where you should go. Girl Scouts is Middle America. That is where the action is." Surprised by his words, but recognizing how right they were, abruptly I reframed my thinking. My eldest son was suggesting that I should take on a whole new, and very large, professional job! Was he telling me that, now that he and his brothers were away from home at college, I, too, was free to explore new horizons? Should I consider leaving the world of private education for broader issues and more diverse people? The next day I called the executive recruiter back, expressing interest.

As I interviewed for the job, I kept thinking of Norman's advice. It would be a gamble to leave my comfortable academic environment, but now, with my sons all in college, I really was free and ready to explore "where the action is." I had no experience with Girl Scouting or Girl Scouts and only an outsider's knowledge of the organization, but knew they were engaged in teaching and learning to help develop all girls, rich or poor. And, they liked camping and the outdoors. Maybe just my cup of tea!

Girl Scouts and their National Executive Director, 1973

A few months later I was standing at the podium in the new Dallas Convention Center, facing 11,000 Girl Scouts and 3,600 accredited voting delegates gathered from across the country to celebrate Girl Scouting, to vote on policies and procedures that would govern its future and to meet their new National Executive Director. The bright green uniforms of the assembled scouts and their strong voices raised in song filled all the space in the convention center with color and sound. A chorus of 460 voices spoke and sang of the hope and faith that brought them there. We watched a film entitled "The Difference is You" while 1500 Texan Brownies swarmed throughout the hall greeting each delegate with a handshake and the message "the difference is you." There were few dry eyes in the house!

Scanning thousands of upturned faces, I was desperately anxious not to disappoint them, but felt surprisingly comfortable—no knots in the stomach, no goose bumps. My audience was super friendly, waving and cheering. They wanted to like their new executive leader. And I liked them already. Their numbers appeared infinitely larger than those I had greeted every morning at Lenox, but speaking to them felt familiar. After all, they were like my Lenox students: girls eager to help themselves, their communities and the world. I had been warned about the "sea of green," but even as I addressed the entire group, I could feel the individuality and eagerness of each person shining through the uniform. Norman was right. Middle America was "where the action is." I felt both fortunate and humble to have been invited to join them.

Girl Scouting introduced me to the informal education that soon absorbed the last decades of my professional life. Historically, all education was "informal" until the advent of British and European universities at the end of the Middle Ages. Today, we would call Socrates' dialogues with his students "informal education." The title of the first Girl Scout Handbook, published in 1912, was *How Girls Can Help Their Country*. It included practical detailed guidance for camping, for health and for homemaking, as well as for botany, sanitation and self-defense . . . and more. And Robert Baden-Powell's 1918 *Scouting for Girls* defined even more activities for girls. Among the badges for which scouting has become famous, he included civics, "automobiling," accounting, industrial activities and even "choosing a career." The education I had known until then, in schools, colleges and universities, was all formally constructed within institutions with defined legal, financial, intellectual and societal accountabilities. I had not yet professionally dealt with all the "informal" education going on, individually and collectively, at home, in libraries, museums, clubs and associations—and even on athletic fields. The first edition of the Girl Scout Handbook described the rationale for including girls in scouting to be their need for "an attractive practical form of active educational pastime"—just like boys. I liked this term, "active educational pastime," finding it an excellent way to describe informal education.

There was much to learn. I started out traveling to visit local councils across the country, meeting their staffs and volunteers, and relishing my first chance to explore the United States beyond New England. Traveling across deserts, farms and mountains as well as to cities I had previously only heard of, I met women reporters whose first jobs in journalism had been for Girl Scout magazines. I visited barrios in the southwestern U.S. where Chicano women enjoyed their first experience leaving home alone (or with their children) at night to attend Girl Scout meetings, and then traveled with them across the poorest to the riches communities in San Antonio, where town leaders invited them to their country club for a Girl Scout dinner. I trekked across stunning open wilderness sites in the West where Girl Scouts camped and explored—and where a park ranger showed us around and served venison sandwiches for lunch. In what other capacity would I be served venison sandwiches from a park ranger's private stock? Attending local Girl Scout meetings, I admired the leadership skills of effective volunteers and felt proud to learn that, in those days, a third of U.S. girls and women had, at some point in their lives, been part of Girl Scouts, as scouts, volunteers or staff.

After these celebratory introductions to volunteers and professionals working out of the local councils in the organization's six geographical regional divisions, I returned to New York to settle down to work with headquarters staff in our large handsome office building on 51st Street and Third Avenue in Manhattan. I was now National Executive Director of a large bureaucracy with a $30 million budget, about 700 staff in our midtown Manhattan office building, another 5,000 staff in regional and council offices, and extensive human and material resources, all there to aid and abet about one million volunteer leaders delivering Girl Scout services to millions of girls. And, for the first time in my life, at the age of 45, I was working in an office building rather than a school, college or academic hall. Some "perks," more familiar in the business world, also came with the job: a corner office on the top floor with its own private bathroom—and two secretaries!

At headquarters, my first job was to learn about the work of my assistant executive directors. Each had responsibility for one of our divisions: administration, community-based services, education, field operations, management information systems, finance and coordination of national board business. Reporting to these folk were directors for fundraising, general services and properties, international outreach, magazines (we had three), membership, educational programming, personnel, public relations, training and government relations. Thankfully, my years at Lenox had somewhat prepared me for work in personnel, education, fundraising and even public relations. For my education in other responsibilities, entirely new to me, wise assistant directors stepped in brilliantly. Strategic planning, now in fashion, was already underway at Girl Scouts. "Values clarification," also underway, reminded me of dealing with scientists and the personal, political, aesthetic, technical and scientific perspectives they use in choosing the questions they ask, and how to answer them. Dealing with the spreadsheets then prevalent in business management also recalled the processes we used in science to record the impacts of different variables on our observations. So a youth spent with science's processes and products was still helping me!

When our board decided that our top priority was to extend Girl Scouting to girls regardless of their ability to pay, my job was to transmit this message of needed growth to our membership through a newsletter and talks to local groups and staff. In staff meetings, as we developed our strategic plan, I suggested framing our mission as "more and better programs for more girls." Again, so reminiscent of Lenox! Similarities to independent schools did not stop there. Girl Scout staff did a fine job of prioritizing services and then building budgets with measurable goals, but their careful planning was often hindered by volunteers who had not been part of the process and whose priorities were to preserve historical programs and attitudes. At Lenox, as in Girl Scouts, developing new programs required testing them against historical assumptions familiar to the organization's alumni and parents.

As chief executive, my daily work kept me far from girls and troop leaders, but local staff kept me up-to-date with issues they faced, such as the "horrendously high" youth unemployment and the neglect of children. They told me that 30% of American families were moving an average of once every ten years. Strained family budgets meant less money available for GSUSA membership fees, while minority groups' needs for services in large cities continued to grow. These problems involved whole systems that required systems-level answers such as providing more food and camp services, always in high demand.

On top of these concerns, the Department of Health, Education, and Welfare released the Education Amendments that became widely known as Title IX. This provided that "no person in the United States shall, on the basis of sex, be excluded from participation in, be denied the benefits of, or be subjected to, discrimination under any education program or activity receiving Federal financial assistance." Did this mean Girl Scouts would have to accept boys? Urgently, we needed to determine whether this law would require us to change our membership policy to admit boys. Following extensive counsel with our legal and board representatives, two congressional committees and the Secretary of Health, Education, and Welfare, we determined that national voluntary agencies were not to be included in Title IX.

Juvenile justice was an additional concern for Girl Scouts and their local leaders. To ensure national policymakers heard the voices of youth organizations, the chief executive of the YMCA invited us to join an ad hoc organization of youth-focused nonprofits to develop and promote the policies we believed could most help juveniles in trouble. Claiming 20 million youth among our collective members, and using this as leverage for some serious Washington lobbying, we were able to offer our various youth services for halfway houses and related activities to help young people in trouble avoid jail. As small groups of us visited key legislators in Washington, DC, men with daughters proved to be our most receptive audience. A few years later, lobbying in the same way for passing of the Equal Rights Amendment (ERA), legislators with daughters again turned out to be our best friends. Academic consultants were also lobbying for juvenile justice legislation, citing relevant evidence from their social science research, so we decided to be sure that academic social scientists included youth agency research in their recommendations. Assigned by the group to pull together the educational, psychological and sociological assumptions supporting the work of youth agencies, I was, happily, back again to a classic scientific inquiry. What are the prevailing hypotheses about juveniles and crime? Which ones had our work validated? What do we know about what works? What evidence-based actions can follow? What do the deliverers of services in youth agencies know, and how can it be useful?

Seeking additional revenue to extend Girl Scouting to girls regardless of ability to pay, our board decided to seek more businesswomen for membership on its national and local committees: an unexpected outcome of rising feminism. Accompanying this objective came ambitions to improve salaries and benefits for the professional staff.

Girl Scouts of the U.S.A. leaders at Buckingham Palace while attending the World Conference of the World Association of Girl Guides and Girl Scouts in Sussex, England, 1975

Developing profound admiration for the skill and dedication of Girl Scout staff, I was surprised to discover that many did not regard themselves as I did: as competitively skilled professionals. Staff was proud to be working for Girl Scouting for the good it was doing in the world, rather than for developing their own abilities and interests. Personal ambition and development was simply not on their agendas. Eager to help raise their self-esteem, I engaged a consulting firm, the Hay Organization, to build a chart of skills and related salary scales for each person working for Girl Scouts, paid or volunteer. Developing a chart of their job qualifications gave everyone a list of their documented skills and experience ("Hay scales") to add to their resumes—and, I hoped, to their self-esteem—and it helped the organization to develop a salary scale.

I was not the only executive with a high regard for our staff. Eugene Hemley, a retired Navy captain, was our chief information officer. His job was to compile a national computer registry of *all* Girl Scouts: an ambitious early venture in computer database development. I remember Gene telling us that, before coming to the Girl Scouts, he accepted the popular assumption that women let *their* emotions interfere with their work. After working with us, he decided that many men with whom he had worked were more prone than we were to letting their emotions interfere with their work!

As I learned more and more about Girl Scouting, it sounded like "girls' liberation" to me. So I coined the phrase "Girl Scouting has been liberating girls since 1913." This was immediately picked up by the editors of the major Girl Scout magazine for its cover headline.

Our bureaucracy was well staffed by skilled and experienced people, while our program activities were delivered by volunteers. Indeed, Girl Scouts' original and outstanding contribution to our culture was its powerful organization of volunteers. However, as girls and women's roles and women's employment outside of the home changed radically in the 60s and 70s, it became increasingly apparent that the "weak link" in Girl Scouting's gigantic chain of people at all levels of the organization was the preparation and training of volunteers: a topic of major concern and attention by regional offices and local leaders while I was there.

The Women's Movement was burgeoning. My introduction to its leaders in New York came when Martha Stuart, a documentary film-maker, invited me to participate in one of her productions: a video on women in management. More new friendships, new ideas and new horizons swiftly followed. When my aide and I arrived at a Manhattan studio for the filming, we found eight other women managers assembled and enjoying a delicious and attractive buffet arranged for us. By the time we were ushered into a recording studio, we were relaxed and warmed up. For our recorded discussion, we were positioned, not in front of cameras around a table, but on comfortable stools of various heights with a skilled camera team discreetly arranged near us. Always using these trademark characteristics of filming, Martha Stuart produced a series of videos called "Are You Listening" in which she addressed critical issues of the day such as family planning and women's rights. The style she chose for filming avoided the "talking heads" format then so prevalent on TV. Martha was a talented, skilled and wise thinker and artist, and we became close friends. I have long mourned her early death in 1985. It was both an honor and a small comfort to arrange for all her videos to be archived at Harvard's Schlesinger Library.

Soon I met other leading New York feminists, and was invited to join New York's nascent Women's Forum. In 1974, Elly Guggenheimer, well-known and much-loved leader of efforts to improve the lives of women and children, brought together this group of prominent professional women. The Women's Forum met regularly, usually in members' homes and offices, chatting "off the record" about both personal and professional issues that bothered, constrained or even helped us. We were trying to create a network for women to match the power of "old boys' networks" in government, industry and academe. Similar groups were soon initiated in other major cities. For each of us, in different ways at different times, lasting friendships and increased confidence in dealing with gender bias followed. For me, it meant the pride of belonging to a new tribe!

Meeting Betty Friedan at one of these meetings prompted my inviting her to join an advisory committee for the Girl Scouts board. Betty and I discovered we had the same birth date and college, although not the same birth year (Betty was five years older). We shared comparable ideas about women's roles and needs, and although I felt closer to the thinking and writing of Gloria Steinem, both of these authors taught me how brilliant writing can have broad and lasting public impact. As I admired and followed the impacts of their writing, I stayed satisfied with my way of advancing feminist issues through working directly with girls and women. Many members of the Women's Forum were abidingly angry with men and male institutions. I noticed that the angriest women were those whose jobs required advancing up hierarchical administrative ladders. They told stories of meeting negative male attitudes that made work unpleasant at every rung they scaled. Having avoided any ladders of upward mobility to scale, my experiences had been different. I had always been a "boss"—even if just a very little one! Starting as a researcher with only one employee (my technician), my assignments led to management responsibility for more and more employees, but not via a hierarchical ladder such as that of assistant to associate to full professor. I had never had to face, every day at the office, a powerful and possibly biased boss who had the capacity to control my advancement or me.

My family had shared some of my Girl Scout life, as they had at Lenox School. My mother came to the reception celebrating my new position, and son Norman worked in one of the departments managing Girl Scout real estate properties while taking a semester off from Yale. While traveling in England with son Russell, I left him briefly to tour by himself while I attended an international Girl Scout meeting at Sussex University. One morning I woke up to find that he had climbed in a window during the night and was sleeping on a sofa in the lobby! And my granddaughter Christina both enjoyed and learned from the UN Working Group on Girls while she was attending a New York high school. What can be better than enjoying one's work and being able to share some of it with one's family?

I was happy working with my staff, proud to be promoting the Girl Scouts' mission and feeling good about positive receptions to my analyses and recommendations. But, sadly, tensions developed with some board members. As a former board chair wrote in a letter to me, "The National Executive Director is continuously caught between the upper millstone of the board and the nether millstone of the staff. The board never clarifies what the NED can and cannot do." Complimentary letters from other board members were most welcome. At the time, issues at home needed more of my time and attention, and I was enjoying a return to science issues and scientific and technological contacts through work on the boards of RCA and MIT. A proud remembrance of my time with GSUSA is a large pillow cover on which a delegate from Sacramento embroidered, for an annual meeting, the words "Girl Scouting has been liberating American Girls since 1913," my name, and a likeness of the cover of the first Girl Scout Handbook. When I resigned from my job and left Girl Scouting in 1975, the one gift I asked for was to keep this pillow. To this day it hangs in its own special place on my office wall.

6

BREAKING A CORPORATE CEILING

*The poet Keats said that science unweaves the rainbow.
I find the unweaving just as beautiful, beautiful in a
different way.*

—JONAS SALK

ALMOST AS SOON AS I took the Girl Scout job in 1972, I was surprised by invitations to join corporate boards. New nationwide concerns about a paucity of women in top business management drew attention to their even more striking absence on corporate boards. At that time, only one in six Fortune 1300 companies had a female director. As this news reached the public, pressure on corporations to elect more female directors grew, and executive search firms were engaged to find qualified women. When recruiters discovered how few "qualified women" there actually were in top management in business, they turned to candidates in the nonprofit world. Progress was slow until strong voices arose in support of this cause, the most dramatic of which was Wilma Soss. At a 1949 U.S. Steel stockholders' meeting, she came dressed in a Victorian costume, saying her outfit represented "management's thinking on stockholders' relations."

In 1960, she came to a CBS stockholders' meeting dressed as a cleaning lady, complete with mop and pail. She had come, she said, dressed to "clean everything up!" Felice Schwartz was another strong voice supporting such "cleaning up" and founded the organization "Catalyst" to strengthen the numbers and the voices of women directors. She soon brought even more attention to the cause when she suggested that businesses create a "mommy track" for women who could not, or would not, climb the ladder to the top!

Apparently, my nonprofit management experience and academic credentials put me on the "qualified" list. The first two invitations to arrive were from Avon and RCA. While having no business experience, I did have science connections to both these companies. I had presented my microscopic studies of skin at meetings of dermatologists and cosmetic chemists, and had known RCA well through Dr. Hillier and my beloved RCA electron microscope. Well aware that I lacked any business knowledge or experience, I relished an opportunity to gain some. With my two eldest sons away at college, I was sure that accepting these invitations would not conflict with family time, but did not know how my GSUSA board would view taking on such additional assignments. Consulting with members of that board, I learned that they considered these invitations an honor and believed that such business relationships could add positively to support for Girl Scouting, but suggested that I accept no more than two board invitations.

RCA Board of Directors with new member Cecily Selby standing next to Chairman Robert Sarnoff, 1972

RCA's world leadership in science and technology made the RCA invitation particularly exciting. As its lone female director I would be following Mildred McAfee Horton, former president of Wellesley College who had, in turn, followed RCA's first female director, Josephine Case, daughter of one of the founders of RCA. It was after Mildred's retirement that I was nominated by the board, and then duly elected by the shareholders. My long term as an RCA director extended through the company's controversial diversification into frozen foods, rental cars, carpeting and publishing. It lasted through the terms of three chairs, from Robert Sarnoff's resignation in 1975 until the 1986 merger with General Electric.

I was equally delighted to accept the invitation from Avon, an important company for women's cosmetics, since the focus of my earlier research studies had been the structure and function of skin cells. Serving as Avon's first female director also gave me an opportunity to advance the participation and leadership of women in a company that markets entirely to women. My tenure on Avon's board lasted until my retirement twenty-five years later at age 70. By that time, six of Avon's thirteen board members were women, and leadership for and by women has remained characteristic of Avon. Andrea Jung became president in 1998, the year after I left. She led the company for years, during which time she and I often met, as her daughter and my granddaughter were classmates at school. Professional women's networking was becoming intergenerational!

As a member of RCA's board, I was also nominated and elected to join the board of NBC, a wholly owned subsidiary of RCA. In the 1970s, each RCA board meeting included a presentation and discussion of NBC operations, including its news coverage. David Adams, who had been the trusted advisor of David Sarnoff, RCA's founder, was chairman of NBC when I joined in 1972, and Julian Goodman was president. These two very interesting, outgoing gentlemen loved news and, in those days, had the funds to operate with ample budgets. With the funding of news coverage not as constrained as it is today, they spent time at each board meeting talking to us about news operations. My son Bill was then a TV news reporter, and I especially relished this contact with his work. It did not take me long to explore my new company's skills in communication to help my own work. I was trying hard to popularize science, so why not try to find out how a formidable leader of TV media might succeed in doing so? I sought a meeting with Fred Silverman, then president of NBC's entertainment division, to ask how he would market science literacy? His answer was abidingly useful: "Find a prime time star who cares about your issue, and persuade him/her to influence the show's writers to include it in their scripts." So often since then have I noted the strong political impact of causes highlighted within prime time scripts, but have never found myself producing TV stories, where I could, directly, use his advice!

Marketing cosmetic products, not news and electronics, was the issue for Avon board meetings. Although my knowledge of skin biology told me how much, and how little, the application of surface creams could accomplish, I became a happy lifetime user of Avon's skin products! Learning of the company's large team of consulting scientists and dermatologists, and of their successes in quality control, I had confidence in their products. Avon's particular interest for me was that the numbers of Girl Scout leaders (about a million) were comparable to the numbers of Avon sales representatives. Recruitment of Avon's field force of door-to-door sales people was central to its business, as was management of a volunteer field force for Girl Scouts. Avon's long history of employing only women in its sales force was born of the founder's insight that women home alone during the day would rather talk with a female than a male door-to-door salesperson. For both organizations, the critical task was to manage a leadership team and its staff nationally, while at the same time managing the field force locally. Affiliated with both organizations, I was soon able to prompt the sharing of "best practices" in field operations between them. In each case, local sales representatives, like troop leaders, were expected to exhibit a certain degree of entrepreneurship and independence while maintaining strong organizational identities.

Most corporate board business is conducted through committees where dialogue and discussion is more informal than at board meetings. At Avon, I briefly chaired the Nominating Committee, where I could aid and abet the board's commitment to increase the complement of women: adding one female within the year and additional numbers year after year. Science literacy was certainly useful in Audit Committee meetings, when we reviewed environmental audits. At RCA, I chaired the Corporate Responsibility Committee where, at last, I was the one on the committee with considerable experience in the nonprofits to whom they made charitable contributions! The excellent staff of this committee worked hard to keep all committee members informed, even providing each of us with subscriptions to *The Chronicle of Higher Education.*

Most committees require staff work to keep the members informed, sometimes hiring outside consultants for this purpose. For its Personnel Committee, RCA engaged executive compensation consultants to provide information on salary ranges at comparable companies. This information was to assist board judgment in approving its own executive salaries. At the meetings I attended, we reviewed tables showing the salary ranges at comparable corporations presented in quintiles, ranging from the salaries of those whose compensation was in the lowest quintile to those earning the highest. Studying these charts in a committee meeting, I found myself readily joining others in recommending that our company should continue to rank in the top quintile—for the reputation of the firm and the happiness of the executive! As individual corporate salaries were moved to the top quintile, the salary range of this quintile could only increase and increase! It soon became clear that this practice was, and still is, supporting our nation's increasing escalation of top management salaries, and thereby, inequalities right down the line.

Despite the many commonalities I was finding between my for-profit and not-for-profit worlds, one abiding difference remained: money! Attending my first Avon board meeting, I was delighted to discover a $100 bill in an envelope by my place: the first time I had ever been paid for attending a meeting! Well I remember showing it off to my husband and son during dinner that night. At that time, both boards paid us directors at each meeting, although soon the practice changed to a yearly stipend, when checks came by mail. Not only salaries, but corporate expenses were much more generous, as I learned when enjoying first-class travel to trustee meetings in the foreign countries in which our companies operated: Brazil (RCA), and Japan and China (Avon).

My first dinner with Avon board members turned out to be a very good beginning. In 1972 in Los Angeles, this was probably the first business dinner each director had shared with a female colleague. Some discomfort was evident as dinner conversation started slowly, but relaxation set in as soon as cigars were passed around after dinner. I took one. My husband was a devoted cigar smoker, so I sometimes joined him, actually knew how to smoke—and really did enjoy the flavor! That I smoked a cigar with the men became a press story and is now part of the annals of Avon. As are the first words out of the mouth of the Avon CEO who ventured warily into Girl Scout headquarters to invite me to join the board. He looked glum on greeting me until he smiled and said, "Oh, I see you wear lipstick. That's good!" Small gestures and a sense of humor are the best way to break cultural barriers!

Following the biological model of survival through adaptation, I always did try to "fit in." This comprised lots of factors, including dress, manners, jokes, habits—looking back at a photo that was taken at my first RCA meeting, I noticed I'm wearing a more colorful dress than I would have chosen if I had had time to shop! "Dressing for business" at board meetings meant modest necklines, dark colors, and never the "informal" sneakers and jeans that were the custom in my laboratory life. For behavior, I tried to mimic the behavior of board members I admired. One of these was Peter Peterson, who would listen to a complex financial report and then graciously ask, "Please refresh my memory. Did you say…?" Then he would pick up on some financial detail in a way that revealed the weakness of the presentation, its need for more analysis, or reconsideration of an action. Another effective director would shift position, lean back in his chair (sitting next to him, I could tell when this was coming), make some light remark and then zero in with a suggestion that would go to the heart of the matter under discussion. Both men had the skill to provide wise financial analyses, and the style to do it in a laid-back gentlemanly manner—usually accompanied by a joke, a humorous remark and a football metaphor. A football metaphor was something I never could attempt.

In each of my companies, my fellow board members appeared to adapt well to working with me, a colleague so different from them in many ways. Being female, the lone female, was the most obvious difference, but, 45 years old when I joined, I found other differences to be the most significant: I was the youngest, the only Democrat and the only scientist! But, as I expected, I was treated graciously and with respect, by board members of both companies. Occasionally there were comments such as when, in the early 1970s, a veteran Avon director could not help making remarks such as "Oh Cecily, you and your feminist ideas" and sometimes "You and your tax and spend Democrats." Such remarks bothered me more than illuminating individual biases, because I felt that my prime job was to help men *enjoy* and *value* working with a woman—to enjoy working with me—for the sake of all the women who I hoped would follow. Living with three sons and a husband, I was not unaccustomed to working with men. Opening doors wider for those who would come after me was, I believed, what I could do was to help the Women's Movement.

Board meetings are for discussions about policy and for action, not polemics or personal comments. The effectiveness of a director of any board relates directly to the quality of the questions he/she chooses to ask. Far too often corporations (profit and nonprofit) are damaged or destroyed by negligent board leadership, leadership that leaves the right questions unasked, and the wrong questions acted upon. The culture of the company and its meetings strongly influence which questions are asked, and which ones are not. In my early years at RCA, when it was caught up in acquisition fever, there was a resounding absence of challenge to such acquisitions from board members. More hard questions from the board might have helped RCA remain an independent company rather than merging with GE.

So often was I asked, "What is it like being the only woman at board meetings?" Well accustomed to being the lone female, I thought the more significant question would have been, "What is it like being the only one without business experience . . . and often the only Democrat!" Although I had plenty of experience at Lenox and at GSUSA with balance sheets, profit and loss statements and audit reports, I did not have the daily contact with business issues that made up the working day of other board members. Nor did my normal day include financial and personal gossip about people and happenings not recorded in newspapers. Business topics were not second nature to me as they were to all other members of both RCA and Avon boards. The more significant question, which I was never asked, should have been, "What was it like to be the only scientifically and technologically literate person at board meetings?" My answer would have been "distressing." While it was surprising to have no women serving on the board of directors of a company whose business was based upon serving women's needs, it was, to me, even more distressing that a company like RCA, driven by scientific and technological research and development, had no board members with more relevant science and technology experience than I could offer. The shareholders, and the company's competitive position in electronic enterprises, would have been better served by directors with more, and more diverse, sci-tech market judgment. Both RCA and Avon had ample experienced staff to handle the scientific and technical aspects of product development, but, at the level of corporate policy, there were questions I knew should have been asked and I might have done so if there had been another sci-tech person on the board for support. Our meetings often included expert staff demonstrations of new technologies and new products. It was there that I first saw a flat screen TV and other new digital technologies, but the absence of critical discussion and appreciation by the board must have been discouraging and disappointing to those demonstrating their skills and products.

Concerned about this absence of sci-tech literacy in management, not just at RCA, but elsewhere, I asked the dean of the Harvard Business School (when my son Norman was enrolled) why courses (beyond an elective) in the management of technology were not included in the Business School curriculum. His answer was that technological management was the role of the engineers, already enrolled in the school. At MIT's Sloan School of Business, where my son Bill was enrolled, courses in business and technology were then offered by a Sarnoff professorship in technology and business—funded by RCA. These courses were not required for all students, however. The prevailing attitude at that time in the early 1980s was that science is just a technical issue so leave the technical details to the technical staff, and let the board focus on financial and legal issues.

In the last year of RCA's independent operation, 1985–1986, before its merger with GE, the RCA Video Disc was unable to compete with other disc designs in the market place. This was a prime technical and financial disappointment for the company. Thanks perhaps to the influence of James Hillier, the designer of the RCA electron microscope and then head of the company's research lab, the RCA design used a stylus to read the grooves on a disc through an electrostatic process, the same process used in electron microscopes. I still have a recording machine developed to read these discs and a collection of discs recorded from RCA's audio library. However, this financial and technical investment quickly went to the scrap heap when the electromagnetic recording initiated by other companies demonstrated the much greater accuracy essential for future optical recordings. RCA's product development engineers soon discovered that their process was not, technically, accurate enough for prime time. Eventually, the RCA Video Disc was abandoned. The company's merger with GE soon followed.

With respect to the "woman's point of view," the ostensible reason for adding women to boards, there certainly were times when it was not only needed, but essential. During a board discussion of Avon's new markets in Japan, I asked how the company was adapting its sales approach to the very different culture and sociology of women in Japan—an obvious question that had been considered at lower levels of management but had not yet been acknowledged at the top. Staff thanked me profusely for getting action at the top. And, at home in the United States, when Avon promoted jobs in its sales force "to provide good things for you and your family," I suggested a more contemporary motivation would be to provide personal and professional development for *oneself as well as* things for one's family. A new thought then, this is now the central theme of Avon's recruitment message.

During my early years with Avon, the company's top managers were all men, so one had to go lower down in the organization to find women's questions dealt with. When there were virtually no women in top management, the few women on boards or in upper levels of management were often the only ones to bring women's issues to the surface. In addition, women directors were often helpful as role models and mentors—and friends—to women in management. As women climbed up to higher positions at Avon, the company slowly but surely became a genuinely "co-ed" company, and an increasingly successful one. As more and more women advance in management, I have noticed our personal lives coming out of hiding. Now I find them much more publicly shared within our academic, legal, financial or corporate lives.

Directors chosen for their gender, race or ethnic diversity have, demonstrably, contributed a wide range of knowledge, talents and points of view to board deliberations. We are increasingly recognizing that diverse people asking diverse questions add value to virtually any and all problem solving. Those coming from different cultural and educational backgrounds often ask questions in ways that are novel to us. Thereby, they can seduce more informative answers from nature in science, and also from society, law, art and finance. With delight, I observe this idea steadily growing in acceptance.

Diverse information and influences from board experiences can help members' own companies. My board experience directly helped the Girl Scouts organization. RCA board meetings were always followed by a lunch in the president's private dining room where I usually I sat next to Robert ("Bobby") Sarnoff, enjoying lunch and the accompanying wine and discussions. Returning afterwards to my office, full of new information and ideas, I had interesting tales to tell of lunch conversations. One day, Bobby described to me, as an interested colleague, that, as chair of the Boy Scouts Public Relations Committee, he planned to help promote Boy Scouts with the motto "Join Scouting, Be a Boy Scout." I returned to my office, worried about whether it was OK for Boy Scouts to "own" the word "scouting." I conveyed this information to my board and legal counsel. After some research, our counsel told us of a 1919 court decision assigning "scouting" to both girl and boy scouts. To consolidate our equal claim, we ordered our bakery to produce a batch of cookies with the name "Scouting" written on them! Subsequently, at a friendly summit meeting between our chair and the Boy Scouts chair, they agreed that "scouting" belonged to both organizations, and "Join Scouting, Be a Boy Scout" was never born. The interlocking board relationships that helped share vital information throughout the business world was now helping the nonprofit world.

Interlocking relationships among leaders of nonprofit organizations can also add value. Meetings called by Bill Aramony, CEO of United Way, to gather the 17 organizations receiving the most money from United Way were a great place to learn about other organizations and their leaders. The first one of these annual meetings I attended was in Puerto Rico. The invitation promised swimming and tennis at our downtown hotel, so I brought along my tennis racquet. At our first afternoon break, Vernon Jordan, then chief executive of the Urban League, turned to our group and asked, "Tennis anyone?" Since I was the only one to take him up on it, tall, handsome, black Vernon and shorter, freckled, middle-aged Cecily went off to the tennis courts. We made quite a vision of contrasts out there. Workmen fixing the outside of an adjacent building several floors above us stopped to watch. As a longtime tennis player, I was happy to help Vernon, a tennis beginner, with practice on serving and rallying balls. He told me that he welcomed this practice since the Kennedys had invited him to play with them. When we all gathered later for the cocktail hour, Bill Aramony asked Vernon about our game. Vernon immediately replied that it was great and that I had beaten him. From then on, I was treated with great respect by Aramony, who had previously ignored this new female Girl Scout executive. In a later aside, he said to me, "I really give you credit—for allowing the Girl Scouts to beat the Urban League!"

My pride in earning a Ph.D. from MIT went off scale when, in 1974, I was invited to lunch with the institute's chair, Howard Johnson, who then invited me to become a member of its corporation. The institute board's Executive Committee deals directly with administrative and financial issues, while the corporation deals with departmental and academic issues. Through their skillful, humane and intellectual leadership, Howard Johnson as chair and Gerald Weisner as president of MIT showed me how an academic institution can and should be led. As I grew to know and work with Jerry, I learned about the brilliance of his leadership. He initiated and fundraised for the institute's leadership Program in Science, Technology, and Society (STS) and, later, its extraordinary Media Lab. STS was born when he decided that an anthropology department should include the study of technologically advanced cities and societies. The Media Lab resulted from the digital media initiatives of Nicholas Negroponte, Seymour Papert and others, and thanks to Jerry's fundraising and leadership, it is now a world leader in research on digital technologies and their human interfaces. Howard and Jerry also accomplished wonders in advancing female scientists and engineers professionally. They identified talented young women faculty, such as Margaret MacVicar, Shirley Jackson and Sheila Widnall, and appointed them to important board committees. These experiences increased their confidence, skills and prominence. Eventually, prominent appointments including heading federal agencies and university presidencies came their way. And in asking me to chair the board's Humanities Visiting Committee, he did the same for me. Throughout the following decades, I have remained proud of MIT's ability to maintain a capacity to mix and match "bottom up" and "top down" talent and initiative. And, I am especially proud that my son Bill and a step-granddaughter are now MIT alums!

With a life now so full of valuable experiences as a trustee, I like to look back to my very first meeting of a board of directors: that of a small Manhattan private school. Miss Green, at Lenox, had recommended me for this position in the 1960s. Since then, service on larger and more diverse boards followed: Brooklyn Law School, MIT and Girls Incorporated in the 1970s, and then Radcliffe College, the Woods Hole Oceanographic Institution and the NY Hall of Science in the 1980s. Each board service provided unique knowledge of organizations from the outside in. Each experience provided lessons about board functions, both positive and negative. My corporate experience with RCA and Avon has certainly helped me become more effective in teaching and in other management responsibilities. At the dinner celebrating my years with RCA, I spoke to the corporate board members present of my strong hope and recommendation that corporate boards invite more academics to serve with them. More mixing and matching of our modes of inquiry, of issues in finance and politics, sciences and the arts, could only help us all.

7

Dr. Selby Goes to Washington

*To look for a black hat in a black room, you have to believe
it is there.*

—*Karl Popper, Philosopher*

After resigning from administrative leadership of GSUSA in 1975, I
had welcome time to concentrate on the boards of MIT and Brooklyn
Law School, and the corporations of RCA and Avon. Time with family
in my home was becoming rarer and rarer as each son started on his
own independent career path. The divorce I had initiated from my
husband was underway. Thus, I started considering possible jobs for
my future. After sixteen years of managing not-for-profit enterprises
and serving on boards of two major corporations, I was dearly missing
being with science and scientists. I was far too long away from research
to be able to return, but wondered whether I could find a way to re-en-
gage with science.

Within a few months, an unexpected phone call offered just that
opportunity. The strong male voice on the phone introduced himself as
Endicott Peabody, calling me from Washington, DC. Recognizing his
name, I realized I was talking to the scion of two old and distinguished
American families, a former governor of Massachusetts and a popular
Democrat. He told me that he was calling as president of a nonprofit
Washington-based organization called "Americans for Energy Independence" and was looking for a candidate to succeed him. He suggested
that my academic background in nuclear physics, in education, and in
running a national organization should prepare me well for this job.
Would I be interested? When I responded that I was interested and
would like to know more, he invited me to come to Washington to

meet and talk with him and other board members. Impressed with the invitation, with the person extending it, and with the organization's involvement with the U.S. government and physics, I accepted this invitation. With high anticipation, off I went to Washington to explore a job that I hoped would bring science back into my life, and introduce me to a world I knew virtually nothing about: government.

I met Mr. Peabody (called "Chub" by all) and members of the board of Americans for Energy Independence (AEI) at their Washington headquarters, where they told me that their organization's purpose was to educate the American public about the nation's energy problems and to address these issues by promoting conservation, coal and nuclear energy. I agreed with their goals and liked their focus on "educate" and "nuclear." Fondly remembering nuclear physics from my undergraduate years at Harvard, I was flattered and excited by their invitation to join this group as president.

Given that all my work since leaving research had been "educating," and nuclear physics was the science I studied most in college, I felt somewhat prepared for the job. I thought, and hoped, I would be able to bring the perspectives of my work on public understanding at Girl Scouts to national energy issues at AEI. I was impressed by the professional skill, experience and commitment of each AEI board member. That Hans Bethe, Nobel Laureate in physics and beloved by physicists worldwide, was a member of the board was important to me. Bethe had emigrated to the U.S. in 1935, and spent the rest of his career as a Cornell professor engaged in nuclear physics research and teaching and participating in development of the atomic bomb in Los Alamos during World War II. Robert Nathan, who had helped President Franklin D. Roosevelt craft Social Security and New Deal programs, was also an active board member. Union leadership was well represented by Joseph Keenan (AFL-CIO leader) and I. W. Abel (Steelworkers). The founder, Zalman Shapiro, employed by the nuclear division of Westinghouse, was the only board member directly affiliated with the production of nuclear reactors.

Mourning the recent death of my father, who had lived and worked in Washington for twenty years, I was attracted to the possibility Washington offered to follow him and his focus on science and society. So, in 1976, I headed to Washington, ready for a new town and a new set of colleagues and friends. I would be testing the wings of my own independence while promoting my country's independence from Middle East oil! Coming from busy and intensely multi-cultural New York, the relative homogeneity of Washington's landscape, its architecture and the people in its streets and offices provided an aesthetic and peaceful change of environment. I enjoyed the spaciousness and scale of Washington's buildings and monuments: no industry or factories in sight. I decided to start my new life as a "single woman" by renting a one-room studio at the Watergate. I remembered my father pointing to the handsome large Watergate Complex, shortly to become infamous as the site of a presidential scandal, and saying, "That's where the rich and powerful live." I thought he would have enjoyed the image of his not so "rich and powerful" daughter living there, and knew I would enjoy the relief of easy housekeeping provided by the grocery and drug stores in its basement mall.

My offices were now just a walk away, as AEI was moving from Arlington across the Potomac River to nearby Connecticut Avenue. After living for a few months at the Watergate, the readiness with which friendships are forged in a town full of temporary residents brought me an invitation to "house sit" an elegant red brick Federal-style house and garden in Georgetown. A new friend and colleague, Joan Martin Brown, a prominent Washingtonian and environmentalist, introduced me to the owners, who were away for an extended period and invited me to live in their beautifully furnished house, with garden and guest cottage, to provide them some security against intruders tempted by an empty property. Served by a part-time housekeeper and living in rooms with O'Keefe and Roualt paintings hanging on the walls, I could do some entertaining . . . almost living the elegant life of a diplomat, but only part-time, as I commuted back to New York many weekends to keep in touch with my son Russell, who was still in New York.

The first time my secretary and I met in the ladies' room, she remarked with surprise, "This is the first time I have met my boss in the ladies' room!" Her remark struck a chord in illuminating that this was not only a different job but also my first job as a female boss in a thoroughly coed environment! But the differences in this job were greater than expected as I learned the political realities of my new position. I needed new skills to deal with the politics in which I was now embedded. The objective of Americans for Energy Independence was to free U.S. international relations from the political power of those controlling Middle East oil. Using nuclear energy to increase our energy supply should have made this an easy objective, but it was difficult, largely because the American public and its politicians appeared to be more afraid of nuclear energy than of the Middle East.

Shortly after my arrival, in a TV interview on the McNeil-Lehrer Report, I was asked whether nuclear reactors are safe. I answered "yes" because, as I said, I had "faith" in the science and the scientists that designed them. I trusted the evaluation of physicists and engineers I knew or whose reports I read. Thanks to such initial comments, my arrival in Washington was greeted by the headline "Public Trust in Science is the Goal as the Lady Takes Over" in the *Weekly Energy Report* of February 23, 1976. The article reported:

> *The heavy energy issue, as Cecily Cannan Selby sees it, is establishing trust between conscientious scientists and their public. As the new $50,000 a year president of Americans for Energy Independence, the educator-scientist from New York City believes Americans for Energy Independence is the group to achieve that objective. As she describes her job, "AEI is a coalition of academic, labor, consumer and corporate organizations bringing together their vested interests to serve the vested interest of the American citizen. We are at work now on recommended policies that people can perceive as best for them and the national interest . . . . We want to create better communication between scientists and technology oriented people who are working to find ways for more cost-effective energy and environmentally safer energy and the public. Once the average citizen understands the situation and its needs, he will have more faith and not attempt to block such efforts."*

Rereading this last sentence forty years later, it sounds so innocent! I was retreading, from academe, the conviction that the "right" messages communicated in the "right" way can lead to the "'right' outcomes." In schools and colleges, knowledge is the power that is sought, and it is found through asking and answering questions according to the modes of each academic discipline. Science's discipline requires agreement on observable evidence through the processes of scientific inquiry. Perspectives like trust and power lie outside the scope of scientific inquiry. The public was seeking answers through political, philosophic or theological, not scientific, inquiry. As I thought these issues through, I began to understand that building trust in scientific messages among non-scientists requires building trust in the messenger as well as the message. The AEI message required more than better communication between academics and politicians, as I had thought. It required influencing theological, philosophical and political beliefs about nuclear energy. This point should not have surprised me. In choosing to work with an RCA product, I was trusting RCA as well as the engineering of its product. Also, in choosing to use Avon creams, I did not examine the scientific evidence for their impact on my face, I trusted the company that made them.

In this way, I quickly discovered that for Americans for Energy Independence to have a voice in designing the nation's energy policy and planning, its organization must be well understood to be free of pro-nuclear bias. In his May 9, 1976, *New York Times* article entitled "Some Have Faith, Some Skepticism about the Perfectibility of Technology," David Burnham wrote, "Dr. Cecily Cannan Selby, a biologist, president of the Americans for Energy Independence, a lobbying group largely financed by the nuclear industry, appeared in a television debate. Dr. Selby said . . . 'I do have faith in science and technology, proven faith. . . . .' After arguing that the nuclear industry in the United States had very strict and comprehensive safety devices, Dr. Selby said, 'There is nothing else that is so strictly and securely regulated. So it is the faith in this system, and faith in the development, the skills and the development of our technology, that some of the unsolved problems will most certainly be solved by the time we have to address them.'"

Thus, the success of AEI's message lay in lack of public, and oil and gas industry, support of nuclear power. Even so, my belief that broad faith in science's messages about nuclear energy could be successfully promoted by AEI lasted until Bob Woodward, the renowned *Washington Post* reporter, half of the famous team that broke the Watergate story, published an article identifying AEI as a pronuclear lobby. I was bold enough to initiate a call to him to argue that we were not lobbyists. Replying to my phone call, I recall Woodward saying, "You seem to be a very nice and knowledgeable lady, but…" The "but" in his reply referred to the political reality that if AEI was perceived as a nuclear lobbying group, it could not gain the public trust as a messenger of a bias-free message.

Vice President Nelson A. Rockefeller, right, discusses the nation's energy problems and his upcoming address to the National Summit Conference for Energy Leadership with Joseph D. Keenan, Americans for Energy Independence (AEI) vice chairman and international secretary-treasurer of the International Brotherhood of Electrical Workers, and Dr. Cecily C. Selby, president of AEI, 1976/77

Meanwhile, through meeting and talking to government, industry, political and union leaders, I was learning a great deal about energy supply and demand. As president of a Washington "educational nonprofit," my secretary could arrange appointments for me with virtually anyone with whom I should speak. Touring the White House recently, I recognized the Vice President's office where my board member Joseph Keenan and I had sat with then Vice President Nelson Rockefeller to discuss energy issues. Invitations to tour nuclear and coal-fired plants accelerated my understanding of energy issues. The immensity of excavation and engineering of a plant we visited in Texas that was starting to develop techniques for extracting oil from shale was stunning—and disturbing. The enormous underground tunnels being constructed in the mine well represented the extraordinary scale of every energy technology we visited. I tried to understand all the technologies involved and how they worked, and was fascinated to learn that electricity production depended on boiling water. Steam from water turns the turbines that generate electric energy. But in most generators, this steam is simply discarded in a wasteful and inefficient process—as Amory Lovins, a prominent American environmental scientist who promoted alternative energy solutions, helped many of us understand. Feeding the steam from electrical generating plants back to other industrial uses appeared to be an obvious step, but it was slow to catch on.

And I learned how teaching and lobbying are often used interchangeably. They both can include conveying the information that supports a particular point of view. When polls reported that most people in the U.S. did not believe there was an energy problem, I decided they were really saying that the public did not define the problem as the experts did. Time and time again, while attending government and private organization meetings highlighting the crisis, I observed the energy problem being defined through gaps evident on graphs between two lines: one line representing the nation's energy supply and the other its energy demand. I was puzzled to discover that the graphical illustrations of supply and demand were all straight lines. Straight lines described linear relationships, but, I thought, the issues were so full of complexity and uncertainty, how could they all be described as linear? Did the projections accommodate the possibility of new U.S energy sources, increased Russian exports or increased Arabian production? Did they anticipate changes in demand due to change in human behavior or new economies joining the market? And, what if new sources of supply, such as extracting gas from shale, came into production? And what if the Middle Eastern suppliers changed their policies?

Recalling my father's teaching about needing "n" equations to solve for "n" unknowns, I knew that to answer questions about future energy supply and demand, we would need to have equations for all relevant energy. In other words, without sufficient present knowledge about energy supply and demand, we could not have appropriate answers. That the more we know, the more we seem to need to know was confirmed by a question I was asked, informally, by the then head of a Washington energy think tank. He asked what I thought the relationship would be between the public use of a gallon of gas and its price. He did not know, and I certainly didn't know. Perhaps members of the public had guessed at this level of uncertainty when they said they didn't "believe" in the energy crisis. Prompted by such questions, I began to ask whether fear is the best strategy for prompting political support and action. Could my organization make a substantial contribution to solving the energy crisis by finding a strategy, beyond fear, to mobilize public attention? At our next board meeting, I suggested we reframe the whole debate. Why not begin with information about energy supply and demand as it affects each one of us rather than with information only from experts? Why not start, in lay language, to invite the public to seek answers from their own experiences? The housekeeper, the car repair technician, indeed everyone knows and deals with cost/supply questions every day. They engage in gap analysis whenever resources become scarce. They know that the price (cost) of grapefruit goes up after Florida droughts and that the coffee can on your shelf is worth more when there is a coffee shortage, and so it is with the cost and supply of oil and gas. When the next gallon costs more than the last one you purchased, you know there is economic pain to come. Why not just share with the public examples of when and why the replacement costs of oil and gas are higher than their marginal costs—give examples of when the next piece of energy they must purchase will cost more than the last piece they bought, and then discuss how to at least keep costs stable?

I proposed to my executive committee that such a message would attract public support through engagement rather than through fear. I suggested building messages on marginal cost and "replacement cost." When replacement cost (the cost of replacing one unit) rises above marginal cost (the cost of producing the last unit used) of virtually anything, its price will go up. Such understanding is open to and usable by everyone. For an open democracy, is not this housekeeping argument a better and more honest approach to the public than asking them to simply depend upon what an "expert" tells them? And, as part of this argument, why not include all the costs affecting energy demand (economic, social, environmental, health etc.)? Why not plug these costs into analyses of replacement v. marginal cost—or even supply/demand curves? When predictions do not come true, public disaffection with and even distrust of science increases. Thus, I suggested that the argument start with each individual's personal energy needs, move on to illuminate all the costs involved in satisfying these needs and then to satisfying society's energy needs. This, I thought, would provide information about how and why citizens can, individually and collectively, make energy choices that can change the curve of social and economic cost projections. And, it would be the best way to position nuclear energy societally through consideration of all its costs and benefits. Fundamentally, I was promoting a more bottom up approach that would enable people to feel engaged and, thereby, supportive.

But these suggestions came too late. The organization had already decided it could not raise the funds to initiate the plans, particularly of writing reports, it had when I was hired. By this time, the plans for increasing public understanding of nuclear energy that I was hearing around Washington sounded to me more like advertising than education. Americans for Energy Independence's direct and immediate need was to persuade Congress and political leaders to advance the country's energy independence through advancing nuclear energy and conservation. Without an extensive educational campaign, political influence was limited to lobbying. Since I was still an educator, not a lobbyist, advertiser or marketer—much as I could respect their skills—I decided that Washington was not to be my long-term career choice. This was the right time to leave because the board was also being forced, for economic reasons, to pull back its ambitions. The members had decided that their earlier objective of building a national network through regional offices was beyond any possible fundraising potential.

My resignation from the presidency of AEI was a friendly parting, much cheered by kind words of regret from physicist Hans Bethe and others. I had enjoyed the liveliness and the proximity-to-power of the politicians and politics with whom I had been engaged. But, I did not have, or choose to have, the hunger that is required to actively seek political power. I preferred working with ideas that are open to reconsideration and analysis. I was an academic, not a politician. I left with no regrets. I had met great people and made good friends, and I would learn that the educational causes on which I spent most of the next twenty years required the marketing and public relations strategies I had learned in Washington.

After staying briefly in Washington, in early 1977, as a consultant in the Department of Commerce, I returned to New York. Before I left, I was scheduled for an interview with the undersecretary of the Department of Energy for the position of Assistant Secretary of Energy for the Environment. I was, apparently, a "live" candidate. However, in my interview with the undersecretary, a man I knew from previous contact, I disagreed with his opinion that educating the public was hopeless because "they will not understand." Politely (I am sure!), I said, "I am a biologist and an educator and look at things differently. I believe that a useful public understanding is accessible and essential. I guess the question is whether someone who looks at things a little differently could be useful around here." The answer came when I was not invited to meet Secretary James Schlesinger!

In struggling to frame AEI's message to make it as valid and powerful as possible, I was struck with key differences between academic and political ways of working. The bottom line for academe is knowledge. For politics it is "strategy." After a meeting in which the board decided to start a chapter of this organization in another city, as was my habit, I took out a yellow legal pad of paper and started making lists of what was to be done, and the people who should be contacted. Governor Peabody simply picked up the phone and called somebody he knew in that city and made a direct contact to start the chapter. I was busy developing the ideas and designing the experiment, and he was directly involved in forging strategic outcomes. Moved by that experience, I wrote an article for the *Independent School Bulletin* asking why we spend virtually all of school and college teaching the beauty, efficacy and history of ideas—while what counts in the world of action, of politics of all sorts, is strategy. Why not also teach strategy? I wrote: "Some people choose to work where they can remain knowledge gatherers all their lives, pursuing knowledge for its own sake, the development of more knowledge, or for the power and delight of the development itself...[Others] use knowledge as a basis for action, for decision-making, for control . . . for power. Their work results in action . . . action that achieves goals like power, control, influence and strategy." I went on to write that "many of the weaknesses of nonprofit institutions and the failures of 'good causes' arise from the failure of the people involved to strategize their dealings with power."

Returning to New York after five demanding years with Girls Scouts, Washington politics, and corporate boards, I was met by invitations to speak at schools, colleges and professional groups about energy, women and management. In addressing such audiences, I concentrated on the interfaces between academe and society; between experts and the public; and between social, economic, technological and political costs. I tried to synthesize what I had learned about working across these interfaces in this decade of endeavors beyond academe. And I was also retreading the challenge students had given me in the 1960s, their challenge to the concept that "Father Knows Best." The last one of this series of talks, in 1980, titled "Faces of Eve: the Scientist," heralded my return to science and education. It was also the first specimen of my work that I showed James S. Coles, my 1945 boss, whom I met (again!) in 1980.

8

None Can Keep Us from the Door

The quality of a nation is best known through the quality of its secondary schooling.
—Nobel Laureate Wassily Leontief, Economist, 1979

IN 1980, EIGHT YEARS after I left the Lenox School, I was back in a school again, a tuition-free coed boarding high school for gifted students in North Carolina. Paul Ylvisaker, then Dean of Harvard's School of Education, introduced me to this glorious new adventure in science teaching and learning. I was visiting Paul and his wife, Barbara, in Boston while my son Bill was a TV news reporter at Boston's CBS affiliate. Barbara and I had both met Paul when he was a very popular and effective instructor of an introductory Radcliffe course in government. All of us girls admired Paul for his looks, charm and excellent teaching, and were delighted when, a couple of years later, he started courting Barbara. During our senior year, I well remember a note he left on Barbara's bicycle outside Sever Hall where she and I were attending a class. The note said, "The owner of this bicycle is taken. Paul."

She certainly was, and they married soon after her graduation. Proud to know Paul and his work, I later followed his career and sought opportunities to talk with him[2]. During a conversation in 1979, he

---

2. Later, when I was re-visiting Paul Ylvisaker at Harvard's School of Education, and asked him what world issues he most worried about for the U.S. in the years ahead, his memorable answer was "the movement of people." He cited all the migrations of people across national borders after World War II and their continuing increase across all continents. Some of these migrations, Paul believed, were self-motivated, some were induced and some were conducted for economic, political and/or religious

mentioned that a brand new school for secondary education in science and mathematics was looking for a scientist to become its head. Remembering me as the physics student I was as an undergraduate, he asked whether this position would interest me. If so, he suggested that I contact Wassily Leontief, the Nobel Laureate in economics who had just left Harvard for a position at NYU. He would be able to tell me more about the school.

When I did contact Wassily in New York, he invited me to lunch with his wife in New York's Greenwich Village. The lunch at an excellent French restaurant was delicious, but it was the conversation that captivated me. So well I remember Wassily asserting that "the quality of a nation is best known through the quality of its secondary schooling." The longer I live, the more wisdom I find in his simple statement, while it certainly reinforced my interest in this new school. It was being designed to advance mathematics and science education for gifted girls and boys and became the nation's first tuition-free boarding school for gifted students. Expressing profound interest, I was invited to Durham, in North Carolina, the school's home. There I met Chuck Eilber, former headmaster of Michigan's Cranbrook School, who had just been appointed to be the first director of what was named the North Carolina School of Science and Mathematics (NCSSM). Chuck and I got on very well, and soon he and the trustees invited me to be a consultant for the planning of the school. Absolutely delighted to be back with science and schools, I accepted this consultation immediately and without question. Thus, after one more fortuitous introduction, I came back to the world of science teaching and learning—never to leave it again!

North Carolina's governor, Jim Hunt, and leaders of its two premier universities, Duke University and the University of North Carolina at Chapel Hill, had decided to open NCSSM as their way to advance mathematics and science education in the state. These same leaders were also spearheading the state's enhancement of its "Research Triangle Park" of high tech and biotech corporations. By one vote, the North Carolina State Assembly had funded NCSSM to provide richer and

---

reasons. Sadly, Paul died young, during the 1980s, and thus the world has missed his presence and leadership during the following decades of human migrations.

deeper teaching and learning for gifted and motivated youth. Those supporting this commitment also recognized that to attract STEM (science, technology, engineering and math) professionals to North Carolina industry and colleges, available high-quality K-12 education for their children would be an asset, even a necessity.

Science education was gaining critical attention nationwide. The Chair of the National Academy of Sciences declared, "The decline in science education in high schools may well be the largest, most difficult single problem our country has." And, increasing publicity about the widespread, poor performance of U.S. students in global science and math tests echoed broadly. Additional impetus came from a National Academy of Sciences comparative study of mathematics education in the U.S. and the Soviet Union, which reflected poorly on U.S. science and math education. Those of us involved day-by-day in starting our new school were not alone in our sense of urgency and mission.

During the summer of 1980 we began meetings to prepare for opening the school in the abandoned hospital buildings that the state of North Carolina had contributed. These buildings covered a large block within a residential area in Durham. On one of our first evenings together, holding candles, a small group of future school employees and trustees toured the former hospital operating rooms, discussing how they could be converted to school classrooms and laboratories. From then on, this group stayed involved in the initial design of the school and its buildings. Our cooperation even extended to the night before students arrived, when we worked together putting mattress covers on all the students' beds! Finding that the beds were ready for the students' arrival, but still unmade, with sheets and covers piled up for students to install, we decided it would be a warmer welcome for the students to find the beds already made up for them. I recall the passion, and, yes, love each of us brought to this task. We were doing something constructive to help students! We knew that in opening America's first (apart from prisons and asylums!) tuition-free boarding school, we were opening intellectual and social opportunities previously available only to few. We were engaged in a piece of educational reform for our country, and were determined to make it work.

Devoted and informed support from Governor Hunt was the essential ingredient for our success. As he and I got to know each other, I told him that my physician grandfather had stopped to look for a job in Boone, N.C., while returning from California to England in the 1890s. Typically, with his "southern charm," Jim responded, "If he had stayed, we would have been kin." Politically, this governor had made possible the legislation and funding that created the school, and he continued to give us his time, energy and enthusiastic support. On one of his unannounced visits, he found me on the floor, in the middle of a chart outlining a curricular design I was preparing with the faculty and the director. Governor Hunt attended several of the many meetings we held to identify the benefits we could offer to our students, and the policies and practices essential to achieve them. During these months before the school opened in September 1980, one of my tasks was to set up and manage faculty search committees. Living in a motel during short visits to Durham, my room became cluttered with teacher applicant files. I reviewed all applications, selecting those appearing most qualified and then sending them along to the committees that were making final selections. The criteria that governed my choices were: love for their academic discipline and for their students.

I was shameless in lobbying hard for the school to follow a liberal arts rather than a technical school model. I was determined to remedy the separation between the sciences and the humanities and arts—christened the "two cultures" gap by C.P. Snow—that had long distressed me in my schools and college, and in my corporate experiences. Thus, I welcomed any opportunity to provide students the multiple perspectives of a diverse curriculum. Now I was in a place where I could make sure that science would be taught and expressed in its full societal, humanistic and artistic context. Needing two teachers for each subject for our first class of one hundred and fifty eleventh graders, I sought strong teachers in the arts and humanities, as well as in the sciences. I also opted not to assign departments, but rather to encourage teachers to work collaboratively on the entire curriculum, and to hold interdisciplinary faculty meetings. I also tried to ensure that it would be a "humane" school by insisting that we separate social and academic discipline. "Smoking behind the woodshed" would be treated as a social, not an educational, punishment: it could not be used to reduce a class grade.

Outreach to the local community was critical to the future success and support of the NCSSM experiment. The school affected all of Durham, so we reached out to the community and to researchers employed at nearby Duke University for advice, guidance and general support. Duke professors were invited to join committees dealing with school policies, admissions criteria and teacher selection. We hired "Ginger" Wilson, a Duke University history professor, for social studies and Don Haupt, who spoke five languages, to teach languages. And, we chose Joe Liles for our first art teacher. He introduced students to the variety of media he himself loved exploring. After talking with me about electron microscopy, I found him including micrographs in his classes' artworks. Several of our new teachers had worked at colleges in our area—Duke, University of North Carolina at Chapel Hill, and North Carolina State University—and all those joining our teacher selection committees clearly supported our commitment to engaging a significant number of African-American teachers and students. The twelve teachers hired for our first year enrollment of a hundred and fifty eleventh-graders included four African-Americans and enrolled about the same percentage (30%) of African-American students. Our choices must have been astutely made, because I later learned that virtually all my initial hires were eminently successful and stayed with the school for years.

We opened the school in the fall of 1980 with all students—girls and boys, black and white, rich and poor—living and studying together. Before the opening, I moved from being a consultant to serving as dean for the first year, and relished the student contact involved. At one point early in the first semester, several female African-American students, all from rural areas, asked me for a place where they could meet to work as a group outside of study hall. They said they needed to "talk chemistry over together" to learn it best. I found a place for them, subsequently learning how important it was to give these young women, whose home culture was heavily rooted in verbal communication and storytelling, opportunities to learn the new and foreign culture of chemistry in ways that worked best for them. They succeeded and eventually did well in chemistry. When other chemistry students told me they were having trouble with the so-called "gas laws," I took a look at their textbook. It began with the theory of these laws—a series of principles and concepts describing how gases behave. So once again, I was disappointed, as I had been at MIT, by chemistry texts introducing their subject with a law, a rule, rather than observations, and then explanations, rather than deriving the gas laws conceptually, with some common sense, from such observations.

Our students often told us how they relished being in class with the opposite sex. They enjoyed informal, in-school interactions between girls and boys who each wanted to learn and achieve. The boys said how great it was to be able to talk to girls about history or science, and the girls said how great it was to be with boys who could hold an interesting conversation! The confidence and comfort they felt in their new environment was reflected in the test scores they earned in a national Westinghouse Talent Search within the first few weeks of school: the highest scores received up to that time for a North Carolina population. Our school had just begun, so our teaching could not be given credit for their good scores, but I believe our culture could. Students living in an environment where their ambition is reinforced and their confidence is enhanced made them happier, more efficient test takers! Our assumptions about how to help these young people feel good and work towards their potential were already bearing fruit. So much of my next thirty years of engagement with teaching and learning was inspired by my experiences at NCSSM.

While developing the school during its first year, we had to plan for admitting the next class. We needed to establish formal criteria for admission. Immediately, we agreed that test results alone could not be the sole criterion and that personal interviews were essential. To start the admission procedure and to consider the criteria we should choose, small teams of a couple of teachers and an administrator traveled to two areas—one in the North Carolina mountains and the other along the state's eastern shore. I joined one going to Boone, in the mountains. Seeking current issues with which to engage student comments, I asked about a "hot" local topic: the transportation of nuclear waste by trucks through the state. I asked students for their ideas about disposing of nuclear waste. One answer I can never forget came from a redheaded young man who told me that, although there was no library in his town, his school did have a *Book of Knowledge*. In this he had read that the sun was essentially a giant nuclear reactor. He suggested that, if this was true, why shouldn't we just send the nuclear waste back to the sun? How I loved this example of divergent thinking! When I also asked him if he thought he would miss home if he attended a boarding school, he replied that his father was a truck driver, and thus not home very much, so there was not much to miss. Another question I asked students was whether they had ever thought of a different way to prove the Pythagorean theorem. Several had! One young man told me that when he showed his alternate proof to a teacher, she told him, "That is not the way we do it in this class." I asked him how he felt about this response. He said he was angry, but had learned to "control" his anger. Our school was a place where students did not have to go through each day with such anger.

Another applicant I remember was a young man who lived in the poorest part of eastern North Carolina and came to the school wearing only flip-flops for shoes. He owned no street shoes. He had not yet studied any foreign language, so I assigned him to Latin, as a base for advancement in other languages. When I left the school to remarry and return to New York, this student presented me with a drawing for which he had composed a poem honoring NCSSM as the "School of Light." The last paragraph of the poem reads:

The school has yet to really soar,
but none can keep us from the door.
We will soon ourselves take flight,
having learned from the school of light.

He signed his name on the poem backwards because he had learned, in his Latin class, that this was the habit of a Latin poet. Twenty years later, when I returned to the school for an alumni gathering, he brought with him his medical degree, his wife and their two children. His poem hangs on my wall now. His line, "None can keep us from the door" resonated with me throughout my years in education. The school remains restricted to North Carolina residents and tuition free. It is doing extremely well and has expanded to 680 students, who are enrolled for their last two years of high school.

Perhaps the most agreeable and productive years of my professional life unfolded during my year with North Carolina School of Science and Mathematics. It was exciting to develop the school's innovative learning environment—and it was also exciting to have this chance to immerse myself in a different culture . . . and enjoy different food!

On first arriving in North Carolina, I discovered that fresh sausage biscuits were readily available for a dollar each. Thanks to the popularity of a similar sausage roll in England, these were, and still are, my favorite snack! But it was not only the food culture I quickly came to appreciate. Once I traded motel rooms for an apartment in a small garden development of attached two-story buildings, I shopped at grocery markets where I enjoyed the "southern charm" of the cashier who would look me in the eye with a smile and a gracious "y'all come back, now!" I learned to slow my New York City pace when a secretary would gently stop me as I rushed past to say, "We haven't had a chance to chat lately!" I wasn't completely transformed into a country girl, however. This was also a year of building up a large bank of Eastern Airlines frequent flyer miles. To keep in touch with my family, many weekends involved a mad rush to the airport, catching the New York plane only five or ten minutes before departure (quite possible in the years before security checks), and then returning to Raleigh-Durham airport from La Guardia, also usually at the last minute, Sunday night or Monday morning. These commutes did remind me that I was still a big city girl. Passing through city streets during the Manhattan taxi ride, I was always happy to be back in a place where one could find diverse people and activities on every block.

It was during one of these New York weekends that I met my future husband, James Stacy Coles, known as "Spike" to all. At a lunch party she was hosting, a close friend told me, "There is one single man here, and he is over there!" I headed for this handsome gentleman, and soon we were sitting on a love seat together, balancing our luncheon trays and discovering how much we had in common. Spike had spent some of the war years on Cape Cod, engaged in ocean research for the Navy with the Woods Hole Oceanographic Institution (WHOI). When I told him that I had taken a small job at the Oceanographic, after my last year of college, and that this job involved measuring the distance between little "blips" on photographic film, he said, "If you did that, you worked for me." Indeed, he had been the head of the lab in which I had taken this little wartime job. At that time, I was eighteen and he was thirty-two—a young married man with two small children. My social time and energy was taken up by men hardly even twenty—certainly not in their thirties, so I had hardly noticed my boss. However, thirty-five years later, I certainly did! I was delighted when, back in Durham, a secretary told me that there was a "Dr. Coles" calling me from New York. Thinking this phone call might be an invitation to dinner, I answered expectantly. Instead, Spike's call was a polite request for my resume! Learning about my familiarity with Woods Hole and finding out that I was a scientist with extensive board experience, he wanted to nominate me for a trusteeship at WHOI. I was a little disappointed not to have a date, but I did send my resume. However, I soon received a written thank-you note, with an invitation to an opening at the Metropolitan Museum and dinner afterwards. And the rest is history!

9

So Much More Friendly with Two

Only with a united effort of science and the humanities can we hope to succeed in discovering a community of thought, which can lead us out of the darkness, and the confusion, which oppress all mankind.
—Nobel Laureate I.I. Rabi, Physicist, 1955

As *The New York Times* reported, "Cecily Cannan Selby and James Stacy Coles were married at Manhattan's Trinity Church on February 21, 1981." Trinity Church had a long history first as a British church, going back to 1697, and it was chartered by the state in 1784. My new husband had long served on its vestry. How proud and happy we were to marry in this historic place, celebrating with our newly extended family and friends. The six children we now shared were all with us, as was my mother and Spike's sister, nieces and nephew. Embraced by our newly extended family and friends, my college friend, Betty, came from Vermont to sing for our wedding service. My son Bill, then a TV news reporter, gave a Bible reading that so impressed Robert Ray Parks, Trinity's rector, that he asked if Bill had considered the ministry for his vocation! After the service, our entire wedding party walked down Broadway in the February cold for a celebratory dinner at Fraunces Tavern, another lower East Side local landmark. A perfect day!

Rev. Parks and Spike had become good friends, and so our premarital counseling was informal and enlivened by a personal story Parks shared with us about his own early married life. When he and his bride moved into the house provided by his first parish, they found twin beds in their bedroom. Determined to replace these with a double bed, they used up their meager savings to buy one. Telling us this story was the way Rev. Parks chose to advise us that our marriage should not include a commute between New York and North Carolina—that we should live together (in a double bed!) as soon as possible. And so we did.

"As soon as possible" came in May, after NCSSM students had left for the summer. My husband came to Durham to help pack up mementos of my North Carolina year into my small BMW for the long drive back to Manhattan. We brought the summer north with us as dogwoods started blooming in each place we drove through—a true harbinger of our marriage. Our personal and professional lives united as Spike moved all his belongings into my Manhattan apartment. Our friends also soon merged, as he delighted in meeting mine, with their feminist and educational passions, and I relished a social life with Spike's scientist and academic friends. Spike's daughter, Ann Coles, and nephew, Peter Bol, were also devoted educators. When we talked about how, between the two of us, we covered educational issues from kindergarten to higher education, I liked to hear him flatter me by saying that my contributions to K–12 education paralleled his to higher education. I had lots to learn about technology and oceans, as he did about biology and schools. I now had the "older brother" I had thought about for so long.

We quickly decided that Woods Hole was where we wanted to put down roots together, and we bought a house there, just a mile from the Woods Hole Oceanographic Institution (WHOI) campus, henceforth spending all our summers there. The house sat high above the large wooded Oyster Pond, with a lovely view of trees or water from every room. When I heard it called the "Porter" house, I asked if it had been the home of Keith Porter, the biologist whose laboratory had so warmly welcomed me at Rockefeller University. When told it was, I delighted in how the different chapters of my life were now weaving together. I was with a beloved husband in my favorite place of Woods Hole, and would be living in a mentor's former home. I was also back in my father's realm of the Marine Biological Laboratory and the "hometown" in which I had first met science. For each of us, the village held happy memories of family, friends, work and outdoor life.

After Spike's wartime research exploring the physical chemistry of undersea explosions at WHOI, he had remained close to the institution as a very active trustee. My delight only increased as I came to know WHOI and its scientists and engineers. Although Spike had proposed that I join the institution's Board of Trustees when we first met, I had not yet been nominated. According to a dear trustee friend, Van Alan Clark Jr., when my name had come up for consideration, he was asked if I had any money. As he told me, his reply was, "All the money she has, she has earned." How I loved that reply! I was nominated and elected, and so we became WHOI's first Board of Trustees couple. Proud as I was to be Mrs. Coles, Spike said I had a thirty-year professional investment in being Dr. Selby, and recommended that I should keep that name. And so I did, for professional use.

Woods Hole Oceanographic Institution (WHOI) scientist Susan Humphris, trustee Peter Aron, and fellow trustee Cecily Selby on trip to Antarctica, 2004

Ocean science was taking giant steps forward, thanks to new technologies enabling oceanographers to view and photograph, in the deep ocean, hitherto unimagined biological life and geological structures. The most famous of these innovative technologies, designed and built by WHOI engineers, is the tiny three-person submarine named *Alvin*, after its principal inventor, Allyn Vine. This small submarine could explore the ocean down to depths of thirteen thousand feet, making 4,500 dives before its recent rebuilding. Another innovative Woods

Hole scientist, Bob Ballard, was instrumental in developing cameras and remotely operated vehicles that could record images at such depths. Still a member of RCA's Board of Directors, I was proud that RCA was responsible for some new technology these cameras needed. When this pioneering optical capacity was combined with *Alvin*'s diving capacity, stunning visions of the deep sea were recorded by video for all the world to see.

My first view of the clams, tubeworms and volcanic "hot vents" moved me as deeply as had my first view of dividing cells! I agreed when my friend, Michaela, viewing a video of deep-sea life, called the images "spiritual." We speculated about the biology of the gigantic worms and clams the photos exposed, and wondered what this discovery of life in primitive environments could tell us about the origins of life. The new question to ask was, "What is the energy source for this explosion of chemistry and life at the bottom of the ocean?" Recalling my studies of clam muscle, it was exciting to learn that the muscles in clams living off sulfur chemistry instead of oxygen in the deep sea are chemically and structurally identical to those living in our aerobic environment. When this new technological capacity was used to explore and photograph *Titanic*'s undersea wreck, and videos were shared with wide audiences, the complexity of the undersea world and WHOI's new ability to view it escalated public and government interest in ocean research. This gave oceanography a needed boost as until then, ocean research was considerably underfunded relative to space research and development.

Spike was president of Research Corporation for Science Advancement (RCSA), a not-for-profit organization founded in 1913 (at the same time as Girl Scouts of the U.S.A.), to enable academic institutions to acquire patents and licensing revenue for their scientists' legal and business expertise. After many decades as the only provider of technical and legal assistance, when Spike retired from RCSA in 1982, universities were, increasingly, setting up their own offices to facilitate patenting and promotion of faculty innovations. Learning of many patents being filed by university researchers through Research Corporation, I began to better understand the business development in the health sciences in which my son Norman was involved. And, when son Bill was treated for his cancer with Cisplatin, I knew RCSA had helped bring this medication to market. After his retirement, Spike stayed close to RCSA, so I continued to learn about pharmaceutical development when accompanying him at meetings. These were marvelous years for me, sharing interests, friends, meetings and family with a loving husband at home and on the road.

Shortly after our wedding, Spike compiled and edited a volume titled *Technological Innovations in the 80's*[3] for which I contributed a chapter on "Current Trends in Mathematical, Scientific and Technology Education." In this essay, I wrote, "Both innovation and technology can and must be included in our objectives for education for all students." This movement of and new attention to innovation is certainly moving this further and faster than I could have predicted when I wrote these words.

While working on this chapter, I received an unexpected phone call (yet another, in a lifetime of many) from the director of the National Science Foundation (NSF). He was calling to ask if I would be willing to serve on a commission to examine the status and needs of U.S. precollege education in STEM (science, technology, engineering and mathematics). The National Science Board was responding to this statement of the president of the National Academy of Sciences: "The nation that dramatically and boldly led the world into an age of technology is failing to provide its own children with the intellectual tools needed for the twenty-first century." Mobilized to action, the National Science Board, the NSF's governing body, set up this commission with a generous two-year budget. It was to be chaired by William T. (Bill) Coleman, a leading Washington attorney who had been President Nixon's Secretary of Transportation.

Spike certainly shared my delight in this opportunity for me to directly serve my government, so I accepted the invitation, and soon was invited to serve as vice chair. Then litigating the Bob Jones University Supreme Court case (regarding prohibition of interracial dating and marriage and the university's claim for tax exemption), Bill worried that this obligation might cause him to miss some of our meetings and asked me to serve as co-chair, so I could preside in his absence. He considered that my knowledge of K–12 education provided a good balance to his political and legislative experiences.

---

3. Published by Prentice-Hall, 1984

A busy 18 months followed as Bill and I, along with members of our commission, held meetings across the country to solicit regional information and opinion about local STEM teaching and learning. At these meetings, local education and STEM leaders and specialists told us about their current K–12 STEM education, and about improvements needed. Attending all these meetings, I was traveling the U.S. again, this time to promote science, just as I had promoted Girl Scouting more than ten years earlier. But this time, I had Spike to rendezvous with at airports whenever our travel schedules coincided!

The work of our commission ended in 1983 with publication of our report, *Educating Americans for the Twenty-First Century*[4]. At Bill Coleman's insistence, NSF staff prepared an appendix listing and itemizing estimated costs of our recommendations. A one hundred and fifty-page book including our source materials and further information was also published and distributed. Four years later, a two hundred-page book of updated and additional reference materials was published and distributed. Thus, our report presented detailed evidence about the status of STEM education in the U.S. in 1983, and included specific recommendations for improvement.

With this report, together with *A Nation at Risk,* the Department of Education's concomitant call to action, we established the first U.S. federal commitment to science education for all. Two sentences I drafted are my favorites: "Science, formerly at the periphery of learning for a few, must now become center stage for all." And "The Commission has seen convincing evidence that all students (barring special disabilities) can develop a useful understanding of science if they are introduced sufficiently young and skillfully." These two sentences introducing our mandate that science must be for all, and that it must be accompanied by increased and enhanced professional development of teachers can, perhaps, be called my "discovery," my "breakthrough."

Our other "firsts" were placing technology education as a core

---

4. *Educating Americans for the Twenty-First Century. A Plan of Action for Improving Mathematics, Science and Technology Education for All American Elementary and Secondary Students so that Their Achievement Is the Best in the World by 1995.* Report of the National Science Board Commission on Precollege Education in Mathematics, Science and Technology, National Science Foundation, 1983.

need for all students and understanding that teaching and learning are strengthened by "informal education." During our final hot summer of collaborative work in Washington, Bill opened his home for us as we wrote most of the report together. Bill wrote all the footnotes, chiding me, when I mentioned I had not yet reviewed them, that for lawyers, footnotes are the best part. Brilliant in analyzing issues and problem-solving situations, kind and moral at heart and gracious and gentlemanly in style, he deserves most credit for the successful launch of our report.

However, politics reared its ugly head. Immediately after the press conference in which Bill Coleman presented our results, Ed Knapp, NSF's new director, withdrew all NSF funds for its promotion. He told us he did this because we called for federal funding, to match state funding, to carry out our recommendations. One of our simplest and most important recommendations was that science teachers be invited to attend workshops for professional development of their teaching skills and knowledge once every five years. Our estimated cost was $350 million, with the total cost of all recommendations reaching $1.5 billion. As a strict Reagan conservative, Knapp objected to any increase in spending of federal taxpayer dollars. Happily, the executive director of our commission had already funded, ordered and released the printing and dissemination of forty-two thousand copies of the report. The good news is that, thanks to its broad dissemination and ultimate support, our printed report lived on, substantially framing NSF budgets for the next twenty-five years. Its influence increased time, talent and interest in science teaching and enhanced and enriched curricula. Our emphasis on the value of informal science education and on technology education led to the vast increases in NSF funds that followed—for museums and science and technology centers and for schools to invest in computers for teaching and learning. Our recommendation for more and better professional development of teachers, however, took longer (a generation!) to gain adequate attention.

Since the NSF did not fund promotion of our report, Lewis Branscomb, Chair of the National Science Board, persuaded the Carnegie Corporation to enlist my help and provide me an office and travel expenses to help do so. Once more, I was on the road across the country, this time to promote specific recommendations for science and teacher education. Wherever I was invited to speak or interview, I found audiences ready to consider change and improvement in schools and curricula and maybe even in teachers' salaries, but seldom ready to help teachers gain the improved and increased pre-service and in-service professional development they so needed and wanted. Struggling to understand why a need so obvious to us was not obvious to others, I came to understand that there are many who believe that good teachers are born, not made—i.e., that they do not need teaching about teaching. For those believing this, the job of K–12 schooling is simple: just put good teachers with good students (who are also born and not made) and forget the rest. Naive as this sounds, it was, and remains, close to the reality I observe. My commission travels convinced me that teacher education is the "black hole" of U.S. science education. Trying to stem the waste of talent, creativity and money being sucked into this hole soon became a mission of my last three decades of work.

When my husband retired in 1983, he suggested that, to enable us to share more free time I should shift to an academic schedule. I should become a professor. "Yes, but professor of what?" I asked. The answer came through John Brademas, then President of New York University (NYU), who had pushed many educational buttons when he was a member of Congress. He was also a director of RCA, so we often chatted at board meetings, and on occasion I shared with him some of my deepening passion for educating science teachers. This greatly interested John, so he proposed that I meet with his dean of education. I did, and soon came an invitation to join NYU's School of Education as a professor of science education, teaching graduate students. This opportunity was almost too good to be true: I could continue to work on teacher education in my hometown, and I had always wanted to be a professor!

It was an excellent time to join New York University's Program in Science Education. A decade earlier, two post-World War II leaders in science education reform at Harvard and MIT had developed a departmental commitment to teaching about science in historic, political and aesthetic contexts. They added courses entitled Science and Human Values, Science in Historical Perspective and The Scientific Enterprise to the usual curriculum of pedagogy and content. These were my favorite courses to teach. For Science and Human Values,

I used the writings of Jacob Bronowski and their frequent references to discussions with his colleague and my friend Jonas Salk. The writings of Gerald Holton, the Harvard physicist and science historian and another treasured friend, were also included. In the Scientific Enterprise course, I covered science-related government agencies important for teachers dealing with funding and education policies, and for students with their career planning. In classes on Science in Historical Perspective, we considered how to enrich teaching science content with histories of its development.

NYU graduate courses in education were scheduled after four in the afternoon, as most students taking these classes were also teaching in public high schools during the day. By the time they arrived, by subway, at NYU's Washington Square Campus for their classes with us, my students had already worked for a full day. Some had state or private funds for tuition, but most enrolled at their own expense. Their immediate ambitions were to earn master's or doctorate degrees to help them climb up the professional teaching ladder. Hungry and eager to learn more, some science grad students worked over the summer in nearby research laboratories. We soon realized that this "hands-on" lab work was excellent preparation for teaching. It brought them experiences in actually doing science, in participating in experiments. Doctoral students took additional courses in other departments and completed and published research projects in science education. Maura Flannery, my doctoral student, completed a thesis titled *The Role of Aesthetic Inquiry in Biological Inquiry*. Another student, Paul Jablon, worked on and continued to publish on incorporating creativity and drama in science teaching, and yet another doctoral student developed classroom action research. Discussions with these students led me to a focus on scientific inquiry and its relationship to all inquiry that would absorb the last decades of my life.

During these years of teaching, I relished the time and energy I could now spend on pondering the nature of the science I so loved. I soon understood why my predecessors at NYU were determined to engage teachers in the whole meal of science: processes, products and context. Most science teachers have had no opportunities to directly engage in science themselves. In those days, undergraduate courses were of the "cookbook" variety. Research was a privilege reserved for professional scientists. By contrast, English teachers can engage in amateur drama and in play, poetry, fiction or other forms of creative writing, and certainly many enjoy in-depth, multi-faceted experiences with literature. History teachers can travel to historic sites, read original manuscripts and engage in their own historical research. Even math teachers can inquire mathematically, on their own. But, until the most recent generation, science teachers had virtually no such opportunities to actually practice the subject they were teaching.

Finding many misperceptions and misunderstandings prevalent in science classrooms and journalism, I decided to attack the one I found most prevalent: defining science as the application of a "scientific method." Teaching science as a "method" implied that it was a recipe, not the meal itself. I started to challenge this approach by highlighting science as a mode of inquiry, an inquiry similar to but distinctly different from, all other human inquiry. To inquire like a scientist is to frame questions, choose and test hypotheses and test these hypotheses with observations. The critical difference from all other inquiry is that the evidence found must be susceptible to proof and disproof. It must be shared by and agreed to by all. Admiring the skill of those who put complex thoughts into a few eloquent words, I looked for wise words about scientific inquiry in the writings of prominent scientists of my era. I found quotations delicious to me in the writings of Polanyi, Popper, Salk, Einstein. Hoping that these might help teachers affirm the centrality of scientific inquiry, I started collecting many that I liked. With such quotes informing and galvanizing our discussions, my best class in the nature of scientific inquiry developed when I asked each student to describe to the group the process of inquiry as they found it reported in a published research report. Each student had to go to the NYU library and choose a research article in a professional journal, and then describe to the class the inquiry/experiment being reported, and whether or not the inquiry and its evidence were scientific. This self-help lesson in inquiry successfully involved every student, offering a palpable and powerful demonstration of self-discovery in learning.

Through my husband and through Research Corporation, I was getting a liberal education in technology. Studying the literature on the evolution of technology, I was impressed by the writings of MIT professor Derek deSolla Price. He described the history of technology as populated by "unsung heroes with brains in their fingertips who were responsible for major scientific breakthroughs." Price's writings made clear that "more often than is commonly believed, the experimenter's craft is the force that moves science forward." Aware of some of the history of scientific instruments, I began to recognize relationships between technology and the humanities. Half a century ago, Eric Ashby, promoting more recognition of technology in universities, wrote that "unlike science, technology concerns the applications of science to the needs of man and society. Therefore, technology is inseparable from humanism.[5]" Soon, I became a devoted proponent of this point of view. I had quickly progressed from the years when, as my husband chided me, I studied physics at Harvard but knew nothing about how a radio worked. As a young boy, he had built radios, while as a young girl, I was reading "physics and philosophy" and playing the piano. Now, I was interested in the *technology* of physics and saw the piano as an art technology!

Until about the 1980s, the only technology taught in schools was for those in the non-academic track. In public high schools, its subjects were often grouped as "industrial arts," not a popular title for academic students. When computers began arriving in schools, their study was called computer science and considered a separate, not an integrative subject. Just as in my Canadian high school forty years earlier, shop had not been considered an academic subject, and technology studies had no place in the academic curriculum. Nobel Laureate Josh Lederberg, then President of Rockefeller University, surprised me with his answer when I asked him which high school class had been his most useful. His answer was "shop"— mechanical drawing. Josh said, "I was an auto-didact and so could teach myself most science, but I needed mechanical drawing for use in designing my experiments." Thanks also to an equally aware technologist at home, I began to appreciate technology as a way to follow John Dewey's lasting message about "learning through doing."

Conversations with MIT's Jay Forrester, a pioneering computer

---

5. Sir Eric Ashby. 1959. *Technology and the Academics: An Essay on Universities and the Scientific Revolution.* Macmillan & Co. LTD, London. St. Martin's Press, New York. 1959.

engineer and systems scientist, opened my mind to new ways of thinking that were born of wartime engineering breakthroughs. In a 1976 article he shared with me, he introduced the new field of "system dynamics" as "a unifying perspective" with which to address education. He wrote, "The major deficiencies in liberal education arise from inadequacies in dealing with the wealth of available information." He explained how system dynamics can help a student resolve the many contradictions within all the different modes of inquiry taught in academe. He suggested teaching models of "the feedback control-loops" within which all processes of change occur. Excited by this way of introducing students to nonlinear processes, I started promoting this kind of technology education in high school, and soon I was meeting with industrial arts teachers to actively help meld their subject with science instruction in the state's curriculum. We were able to move this change as the result of a state project to identify the desired outcomes of K–12 science education. The old distinction that academe was for brains while technology was for brawn was changing!

"What should students understand and be able to do by the time they graduate from high school?" That was the central question when Tom Sobol, then New York's commissioner of education, invited some state educators to come to Albany to establish student outcomes for K–12 grade schools. Sobol suggested that the best way to determine educational input is to start with the output desired. Rather than asking what curricular content should be, why not ask what should students should understand and be able to do as a result of, as an outcome of, their school courses? And so, I was asked to lead a small group of STEM teachers to suggest the desired outcomes of science teaching and learning. My group included one representative each from math, engineering, biology, chemistry and physics. We had a great time conferring together, and the "outcomes" we ultimately recommended became embedded in New York state's curriculum guidelines for some years to come!

For me, clarifying these outcomes illuminated my entire life with science. How well I remember standing at an easel, suggesting a first outcome and writing it down: "Students will understand and be able to use mathematical analysis, scientific inquiry and engineering design to pose questions, seek answers and design solutions." Indeed, the next two decades of my professional life would be spent promoting and developing these words! Each of our nine recommendations, listed below, defines what teaching should help students understand, and be able to use. The first three relate to the processes of learning; the next three provide detail on the content of science, technology and mathematics to be understood; and the last three answer the "So what?" questions: "What are they good for? How are they used?" We recommended that students should:

- Understand and be able to use mathematical analyses, scientific inquiry and engineering design to pose questions, seek answers and design solutions.

- Understand and be able to use the basic engineering concepts of systems analysis, and their uses in the analysis of complex interrelated phenomena.

- Know about and use a full range of information sources. These may include school and community resources such as people, libraries, museums, computers, business, industry and government agencies.

- Demonstrate knowledge of community resources (people, libraries, museums, computers) and history (physical setting, living environment and the human organism).

- Demonstrate knowledge and skills related to the tools, materials and processes of technology to create products, services and environments for human endeavor (e.g., agriculture, health, manufacturing, construction, transportation, communication).

- Understand and be able to use basic mathematical ideas (logic, numbers, measurement, probability, statistics, estimation, simulation, algebra, geometry, etc.) for problem solving, experimentation, validation and other real-world applications.

- Recognize and describe concepts shared by math, science and technology, and the social sciences, arts and humanities. Examples of such shared themes that can help connect learning in all modes of inquiry include equilibrium, time, evidence, space, balance, order, disorder, feedback.

- Apply the knowledge and skills of math, science and technology to make informed personal, social and professional decisions.

- Exhibit habits of mind and social job-related skills to work productively with others, achieve success in different jobs and seek life-long learning and advancement.

When our work was done, our little group had achieved unanimous agreement, but heard that other disciplines did not achieve unanimity—not surprising news for anyone who has worked on curriculum committees! Two factors contributed to our success: the content of STEM subjects is more readily defined than that of most other subjects, and we had only one person representing each sub-discipline. Thus, conflicts between academic subsets were avoided.

Shortly before our report was released, politics did intervene. The Moral Majority became active in Albany, forcing Commissioner Sobol to change our "outcomes" to "standards." This group's viewpoint was that "outcomes" include "values" but only families, not schools, should have responsibility for values. Subsequently, the National Academy of Science's National Research Council followed suit in their establishment of national standards (not outcomes!) for K–12 science education. And today, the use of educational standards puts the emphasis on outside "expert" determinations of the value of subject matter content, not so much on what the subject matter can help students understand and be able to do.

At about the time I was meeting and marrying Spike, I was invited to serve on the board of the New York Hall of Science (NYSCI), a museum situated in the borough of Queens in a stunning building that had been built for the 1964 New York World's Fair. In 1981, attorney Seth Dubin and some friends and colleagues led an effort to reconstitute this museum, originally developed by this small group of Bronx School of Science graduates. Never having lost his passion for science education, and aware of the burgeoning growth of public interest in the U.S., Seth led the reconstitution and concrete renovation of this standout museum. Today, the New York Hall of Science presents some 450 exhibits, demonstrations, workshops and participatory activities that explain science, technology, engineering and math. It is now well recognized and honored as a national leader in STEM education.

My own education and work in this field ran parallel to the development of this exceptional, interactive museum. Since the 1980s I have served as a trustee and as vice president of its board and am now honored with the title Trustee Emerita. It has been a total delight to be affiliated with the Hall of Science, first led by Alan Friedman and now by Margaret Honey. The Hall brings hands-on, active, participatory, STEM learning to all New Yorkers and visitors. The philosophies of education and science governing its work reflect the best of all my STEM learning over the past thirty years—and much more. In its beautiful building and on its much-expanded site, half a million New York City teachers and nearly a million visitors overall enjoy exciting exhibits, workshops and special programs, all highlighting science, engineering and mathematics inquiry and now featuring multiple dimensions of Margaret Honey's theme, "Design, Make, Play."

In 1993, I suddenly faced a new and different kind of knowledge: my beloved husband was in the early stages of dementia, suffering from Alzheimer's disease. His first symptoms were evident in errors dealing with numbers, as in writing checks and figuring out addresses on New York's streets. More memory loss soon followed, and with it my fears of his losing his way when alone. The summer was coming, so I moved us to Woods Hole, thinking it more comfortable for him to be housebound there. Physical disabilities came next. When it became impossible for me, or even for a nurse and me, to help him out of a chair or out of bed, and with the full support of his children, I was able to move Spike to an excellent nursing facility affiliated with Falmouth Hospital and only two miles from our home. Spike's children visited as regularly as they could and were a great support for their father and for me.

The following three years included part-time commuting between New York and Woods Hole in order to keep up some NYU teaching and to visit my sons, who were all working in Manhattan. During winters in Woods Hole, when the snow fell thickly, I used cross-country skis to travel our unpaved, dead-end road to my car, and also enjoyed cross-country skiing on the pond and the local golf course. For the last few months of this shuttling back and forth, my seasonal Woods Hole neighbors, John and Judith Dowling, who were co-masters of Harvard's Leverett House, invited me to help out as a resident tutor for one semester while a regular tutor was on leave. My assignment was to be a responsible adult, living in a residence hall along with the students and sharing meals with them. John was particularly eager that I represent women in science in the dining room and residential community. Frequently hosting tables of women students studying science, it was a delight to, once again, be learning from young people! Harvard students, on the whole, seemed much more goal-oriented than they had been in my day, and a very high percentage were pre-med. Then, computer science was much more narrow and focused than it became two decades later, with very few women yet expressing interest in this area.

While at Harvard during the second semester of 1996, I satisfied a long-held curiosity by auditing a history of science course called Astrology, Alchemy and the Occult Sciences. I was eager to find out why school texts so often imply there was no science between the centuries of Aristotle (384–322 B.C.) and Francis Bacon (1461–1526). Wasn't anyone asking "scientific questions" about their world for 1800 years? There, I learned scientific approaches had not ceased, but rather had morphed in different directions. Scholars in the Middle East and India had kept inquiry about the natural world alive and had provided substance and sustenance for the rebirth of science, through astrology and alchemy. Eventually their ventures took new forms in Europe's Enlightenment. A key port of entry to Europe for experimental approaches was through occult sciences in the Mediterranean. Increasing my understanding of the history of technology and innovation thus enabled me to use it better and more fully in my years ahead.

For James "Spike" Coles, my husband, a man whose life had been often governed by academic semesters, and who honored academe through his life, it seemed fitting that his death coincided with the end of the semester—and my fiftieth college reunion. Our families, and others who loved him, joined together at the Church of the Messiah, our historic little Woods Hole church, for a service that honored Spike's life: all that he accomplished for the people, ideas and science that he loved. I chose Biblical words for our gravestone: "By their works shall ye know them."

10

SCIENCE IS A PERSONAL AND DEMOCRATIC INQUIRY

Science as something existing and complete is the most objective thing known to man. But science in the making, as an end to be pursued, is as subjective and psychologically conditioned as any other branch of human endeavor—so much so that the question "what is the purpose and meaning of science?" receives quite different answers at different times and from different sorts of people.

—ALBERT EINSTEIN, *1934*

IN BEIJING, CHINA, IN 1995, while representing Girls Inc. at the United Nations' Fourth Annual Conference on Women, I heard the strongest argument for universal science and technology literacy that had yet come to my ears. It came from a Nigerian delegate who stood up at a plenary session discussion to say, "The girls and women of my country, as well as the boys and men, need knowledge of science and technology as much as they need reading and writing." With stunned delight, I was hearing the message we had been working hard to promote in the U.S. now declaimed to a global audience, and in words that could not be denied! A plenary session was called by this conference's executive board to discuss its recommendation that the concluding report, its "Platform for Action," propose that the United Nations expand its definition of literacy to include science and technology. Following the Nigerian delegate's support of this proposition, other delegates spoke up, one after another, to echo her declaration that understanding and using the skills and knowledge of science and technology are essential for participation in today's society.

The Canadian and US delegates did not argue against the spirit of the discussion, but did not agree that it would be wise to change the UN definition of literacy at that time. While acknowledging the value of science and technology, a change, they said, would confuse and constrain current efforts of governments and agencies to continue to collect data about reading and writing literacy in nations and communities worldwide. In response, the Nigerian delegate spoke up again. With her clear melodic voice and standing erect in her brilliantly colored national costume, she expressed regret that all countries did not recognize the need to change policies as the needs of citizens change. Why wait until bureaucracies adapt, she argued, to meet today's needs of girls and women, boys and men around the world? She acknowledged administrative obstacles but argued that the people's *need to know* is our immediate need and responsibility. She emphasized that "we must all make such knowledge available." With consummate skill, the meeting chair responded with a compromise statement. She won delegates' approval that the conference's final Platform for Action include the statement that steps must be taken "to promote scientific and technological knowledge together with literacy and life skills, taking into account current benchmarks and targets." This wording did take an important and historic step forward, but did not fully reflect the conviction expressed at this meeting, notably by delegates from the developing world, that the processes and products (knowledge) of science and technology are now, like reading and writing, essential capacities for human development and participation in democracy.

Commenting on this session, my longtime friend, Michaela Walsh, also attending the conference, suggested to me that the "idea" of science is like the "idea" of democracy in starting locally, and now moving to the global marketplace. Her words struck me with the possibility that "democratic science" might be a great way to describe the science and technology UN delegates had in mind. Wasn't a democratic science the desired outcome North Carolina had in mind when it started the North Carolina School of Science and Mathematics, and that the National Science Foundation sought when it set up our commission on precollege STEM education in 1982? It was what we, at NYU, had in mind in our preparation of science teachers, and it was what the New York Hall of Science was now actively promoting in Queens, New York. And, recalling Hillary Clinton's memorable message at the conference, "Women's rights are human rights," literacy, including scientific literacy, is also a human right, now moving globally. Following Clinton's language, we were saying that *understanding and being able to use science, technology, engineering and mathematics provides life skills that, today, constitute a human need and right.*

Returning to New York and my family, I fantasized that the thousands of delegates attending the UN meeting would, as they returned home, immediately start influencing their local leaders to adopt the conference's Platform for Action! Days spent with women who represented the world's diverse cultures and were unified in their passion for worldwide STEM literacy had left me optimistic for immediate action. Some progress had been made, so it was hard to accept that "immediate action" did not follow.

However, my dear husband's death soon after we returned home postponed such thinking and follow-up action for me. Although a welcome relief for him, his death, in July 1996, came far too soon for me. In July, it was followed, blessedly for me, by the birth of my fifth grandchild, Christina. When 1997 came along, I was seventy years old, and facing what seemed a bleak future without my husband, and without the kind of engrossing and challenging work I had relished all my life. How could I, should I, now spend my time? My sons were wonderfully supportive, but their developing lives and families needed their full attention. My question was answered by female scientists with whom I had been discussing repeating a landmark 1979 New York Academy of Sciences conference on women in science. They asked me if I would be willing to lead it. Delightedly, I answered "yes," particularly happy that, in this meeting, I would be able to follow up on recommendations from the Beijing meeting.

At about this time, I discovered that the founders of modern science, Galileo and Newton, had also believed that science literacy is for everyone! Initially, each had used his common language (not the scholarly language of Latin) in which to report his earliest evidence. Galileo's subtitle for his first publication, *The Starry Messenger*, in 1610, describing the moons of Jupiter was *Revealing Great, Unusual and*

Remarkable Spectacles, Opening These to the Consideration of Every Man, and Especially of Philosophers and Astronomers. This book was a popular sensation. Translated into other common languages, its message reached philosophers and astronomers and "every man" across Europe. In a 1612 letter, Galileo wrote, "Now these people, while provided with a good intelligence, yet, because they cannot understand what is written [in books], retain through life the idea that these big folios contain matters beyond their capacity which will forever remain closed to them; whereas, I want them to realize that nature, as she has given them eyes to see her works, has given them a brain to grasp and understand them." But, about ten years later, he was forced to give up using the language of the people. The church fathers gave him permission to write only in Latin, the scholarly language, and "as a mathematician and hypothetically." Isaac Newton, born in England in 1642, the year Galileo died, initially wrote his seminal *Optiks: Or a Treatise of the Reflections, Refractions, Inflections & Colours of Light* in English for the public. But in 1687, Newton tried to avoid the intellectual and public challenges his work had received by writing *Mathematical Principles of Natural Philosophy* in mathematical language that was almost totally opaque to most of his contemporaries.

So, modern science started off, in the seventeenth century, using language not accessible to everyone. Galileo's "every man" was left out. And women were also left out. Galileo and Newton followed Francis Bacon in using patriarchal language and images in their publications, and the then nascent Royal Society soon followed suit and recorded its mission as to "raise a Masculine Philosophy whereby the Mind of Man may be ennobled with the knowledge of Solid Truths." At that time, in Europe and England, women were participating in science and engineering in convents, in fields, gardens, and in drawing rooms. They were not excluded from the practice of science until it became professionalized and moved into universities that did exclude women and "others." Thus, thanks to sociological, educational and religious influences, modern science began without the professional participation of women—or of the common man.

Cecily Selby at podium at NYU symposium in her honor, 1998. Panelists included, left to right, Pamela Abder, Janice Koch, Paul Jablon, and Julia Rankin.

In planning the 1998 NY Academy of Sciences conference, I kept these issues in mind as I focused the program *not* on adapting women to hostile environments but on promoting institutional change and on developing environments that would aid and abet the entry of women into scientific fields. The objective was to achieve institutional openness to the range of styles, needs and strategies of professional women. I chose conference speakers with real-world institutional, not just theoretical or ideological, perspectives. I asked speakers to focus on problem solving rather than on problem identification. Informal and formal education, commercial enterprises, and all factors (gender, race, disability) causing exclusion from science must be included. The conference objective was to highlight the attitudes and actions needed to enable, nurture and promote more women choosing and succeeding in science as their professions. It sought to address questions like: What are the characteristics that constrain entry and advancement of women? What must change so that all national talent will be utilized? Even in those days, we knew we had to address an anti-diversity and anti-science public and Congress. We also made clear that public interest and needs must be represented and addressed by teachers, professors and scientists.

After about a year of planning, and with the invaluable support and assistance of the New York Academy of Sciences, the conference was held in 1998 at the New York Academy of Medicine's historic and elegant building on Fifth Avenue, facing Central Park. Wanting to highlight not only women's *achievements* to date but also how women's *participation* would benefit science itself, I selected the title "Women in Science and Engineering: Choices for Success." I prefaced the conference proceedings, published in 1999 as volume 869 of the *Annals of the New York Academy of Sciences*, with these words: "Women have always included science and technology in *their* choices and successes. But not until today do we hear voices raised to say, as they do in this volume, that science and engineering enterprises must choose women for their own successes." My preface continued, "Throughout human history, women have created technologies. And some have led in the development of scientific inquiry. Even goddesses of the ancient world had their medical, scientific and technological assignments. Indeed, the work, talents and imagination of women were part of science and engineering's beginnings in drawing rooms, in the field and in convents until they were excluded when such work moved into universities. . . The goals is, simply, to enable good people to do good things. Ultimately, everyone will benefit. One might say that we hunger to return to the equal opportunity of ancestral goddesses who were responsible for health, agriculture, newer sciences and technologies for all."

Each of our male speakers was actively engaged with female students and colleagues in laboratories, classrooms and fieldwork. We hoped that their tales of successfully sharing their science with female students and colleagues would encourage more men to do likewise! I did suggest that speakers highlight the impact of laboratory cultures and scientific styles on women's participation, and on issues of community and isolation. This focus brought new and important attention to workplace issues not previously highlighted in sociological research. In closing the conference, I summarized speakers' extensive criticism of "oppressive" environments in universities, and of educational, organizational, political and social systems constraining access to science for all. Just as studying medical pathologies helps to reveal "normal" organic structures, studying the pathology of science education helps reveal how today's "normal" science hinders diversity.

While I was engaged in editing a conference report, Paula Rayman, then director of Harvard's Radcliffe Institute for Advanced Study (Radcliffe College's successor), called to ask if I would consider spending a year in Cambridge, MA. Hearing this question, I smiled to myself because she could not know how eager I was to spend time there—almost as much as I still yearned for time in Cambridge, England! She suggested that I spend a year at the Institute to plot, plan and develop the advancement of women at Harvard . . . and elsewhere. A most generous friend invited me to live in her lovely house nearby, so I readily packed up some clothes from my Manhattan apartment and moved myself and my car to Cambridge, convenient for occasional travel to either Manhattan or Woods Hole.

In those days, the prevailing arguments used to advance women in science were: human rights, equal opportunity and human capital. Now that I was in Cambridge, embedded in Harvard's and MIT's environments, I recognized that these arguments were, perhaps, persuading male faculty to be nice to women faculty and students, but they were *not* prompting them to share intellectual or political power. At Harvard, there was little sharing of intellectual power with women in departments that, like chemistry and physics, could boast just one female tenured professor.

It was then I recognized that to declare that science is good for girls and women, we need evidence that girls and women are good for science! Although we believe this, we have not presented and substantiated evidence that this is so. We have not been teaching or preaching that diversity in the gender, race or culture of scientific investigators can add value to science. Once I thought about this, I knew what my next project should be: to identify and highlight evidence that *it does matter who does science.* I needed to change science's axioms of inaccessibility and uniformity to definitions that would broadcast its accessibility and diversity. Science is in the business of asking questions, but confusion abides when science is asked questions about itself, about what scientists do and about what makes "science" science. Throughout all my years of hands-on work at lab benches, I do not recall any of us asking ourselves, or each other, for a definition of the science we were engaged in. We only need definitions when we start teaching, or, in our "golden years," when, like me, we find time to philosophize. But now, to promote diversity in science, I needed to determine how and why *who* does science does matter.

My investigation of the nature of scientific inquiry began in earnest while I was a Visiting Fellow at Harvard's Radcliffe Institute. Working with a research assistant, I searched the writings of successful modern scientists for the reasons they give for choosing science, and for choosing how and *why* they do it and how such choices vary with what they believe and what they believe about the power and the limits of science. As I learned in my early Woods Hole years, different scientists choose science for different reasons and choose to practice it in many different ways. This is not always obvious because scientists seldom write about their "private" processes of creation, what really goes on in an inquiry. Only their "public" processes, their successes, are included in research and news reports. What goes on "privately" in an investigation, in reports of Ph.D. theses, is not included; in writing my Ph.D. report, I was not expected to include what did not work—only what did work.

The scientists whose writings I examined all agree that science starts with a question. It is an Inquiry, not a Method. After selecting a question, the scientist determines what kind of investigation could provide an answer. Most investigations start with an educated guess, a hypothesis, about what the answer could be. The next step is to test the hypothesis using a "thought" or a practical, tangible experiment, or direct observations, or using mathematics, or making something to see if it "works." If these tests do work, thereby validating the scientist's hypothesis, and if and when confirmed by others, the hypothesis moves from being a guess to becoming a conclusion. Commenting in 1988, Nobel Laureate in medicine François Jacob put it well, "Contrary to what once I thought, scientific progress did not consist simply in observing, in accumulating experimental facts and drawing up a theory from them. It began with the invention of a possible world, or a fragment thereof, which was then compared by experimentation with the real world."

Originally, simple observations of nature were most commonly used to test hypotheses. Then came experiments designed to reveal "hidden" processes to answer questions. Often, know-how can come before know-why, so experimental design can be a "form of thinking" as well as a practical expression of thought. The role of technicians "with genius in their fingertips" is often neglected when thinking about scientific inquiry—the science of acoustics followed the violin-making genius of craftsmen in Cremona. Watson and Crick's double helix is an example of a "possible world" hypothesis, based upon prior knowledge and adding their dash of imagination. It was first tested by Rosalind Franklin's X-ray diffraction observations, and then, later, by the Meselson-Stahl experiment—and never, yet, falsified. Hypotheses can stem from personal convictions. As feminists, Sarah Hrdy hypothesized that studies of male chimpanzees missed valuable information that studies of female chimpanzees would yield, and Bernadine Healy led the National Institutes of Health to hypothesize that studying cancer only in males missed essential information that studies of female breast cancer could yield. Hypotheses can also be imaginative preconceptions, acts of the particular investigator's mind, like Einstein's preconception of gravity. Constructing hypotheses and deciding how to test them challenges the imagination, creativity, knowledge and intuition of scientists. Testing hypotheses in classroom situations is slowly but surely becoming a common technique to stimulate students' interest and imagination.

While reading the works of polymath Michael Polanyi (1962), I discovered a sentence that, in a few words, explains why "who" does science matters. He wrote, "Science is an interrogation of nature, but nature can only respond in the way the question is asked." What an observation or an experiment reveals is what the observer is paying attention to, or what the experiment is designed to reveal. Nature only reveals its secrets when the questions and the experiments are designed wisely enough to reveal them. The experimental design, the technical skill and the critical spirit of a human being are needed to coax new information and new data out of nature. The broader the perspectives of the experimenter/inquirer, the more information will be revealed.

To answer the question "Is the molecular structure of DNA spherical?" experiments designed to test whether it is a sphere should conclude that it is not. But unless designed to do so, they are unlikely to gather evidence that is a helix. Positive results from an experiment asking, specifically, whether it is a helix provide the only direct way to conclude that it is! In an earlier chapter, I noted that I was advised not to "look for a helix" in examining muscle molecular structure. Not designing our procedures to test for a helix, we could not "discover" that it is. By not choosing the winning hypothesis, we missed the winning evidence, but we did not miss performing good scientific inquiry. As scientists all know, missing winning hypotheses is not, necessarily, bad science. It may just be bad luck!

For the past century, exponential growth in the availability and use of new and more powerful technological tools with which to ask and answer questions has prompted nature to reveal more and more about itself. The history of human development records how human curiosity has consistently invented new tools with which to try to satisfy this curiosity. Humanity seeks useful explanations of what some phenomenon is, what is in it, and what makes it work. For an explanation to be useful, everyone involved must agree on it: the consistency of star positions, the timing of the Nile's tides, the circulation of the blood.

Scientific evidence has long been characterized and understood as verifiable, as open to proof that it is or is not correct. Thus, for science, the answer cannot be just a personal opinion: it must be a shared opinion. In the last century, the philosopher Karl Popper turned this thinking around, arguing in 1963 that the more accurate characteristic is its *falsifiability*: its openness to proof that it is wrong. Thirty years later, in a landmark 1993 decision, the U.S. Supreme Court supported Popper's thesis, and quoted him: "Scientific methodology today is based on generating hypotheses and testing them to see if they can be falsified; indeed this methodology is what distinguishes science from other fields of human inquiry . . . . The criterion of the scientific status of a theory is its falsifiability, or refutability or testability." (Daubert v. Merrell Dow Pharmaceuticals, 509 U.S. 579 [92-101]) The proposition by a Korean scientist that he had cloned human embryos was falsified when other investigators proved his evidence fraudulent. His inquiry was thereby established as nonscientific. According to its proponents, Intelligent Design cannot be disproved. It is, therefore, not scientific.

The more we look, the more we find personal perspectives in scientific inquiry. As Einstein wrote in 1934, "Science as something existing and complete is the most objective thing known to man. But science in the making, science as an end to be pursued, is as subjective and psychologically conditioned as any other branch of human endeavor." The investigator, the scientist, has multiple choices of questions and procedures available to him/her. Scientific perspectives from the scientist's prior work should be prime determinants, but personal experience, prior knowledge—and biases—can all have influence. As I noticed in my Woods Hole childhood, different scientists sensed differently, questioned differently and hypothesized differently. Such differences can be recognized more readily in the *way* people choose to work. Those loving to work hands-on will choose experimental or fieldwork. Those loving ideas may choose to work theoretically. Those who love order will find order, and those intrigued by ambiguity will find it. Modern neuroscience is helping us understand that our bodies as well as our minds are involved in such choices. Dimasio (1994) led in showing how feelings, emotions, biological regulation and magic all play a role in human reason and consciousness. In my recent adventures in modeling three-dimensional figures in clay, I find an explanation of how and why my lifelong enjoyment with imagining three-dimensional structure led to my early delight with microscopy. In every act of knowing there is a passionate contribution from the person knowing.

Scientists are aware of this, of course, and are not shy in mentioning their passions and personal tastes, and often the different perspectives of those with whom they work. Many have discovered their pleasure and the benefits to science in working in groups of those with different perspectives. Peter Medawar (1974) wrote, "It would be hard to even imagine a collection of people more different from each other in origin, education, behavior, appearance, style, and worldly purposes than those involved in discerning the DNA structure: James Watson, Francis Crick, Lawrence Bragg, Rosalind Franklin, and Linus Pauling."

Additional evidence that doing science is a personal endeavor is found in the many happy and eloquent memoirs scientists write about why they love to do science. Max Born (1936), whose writings introduced me to physics, wrote of his longing for "something fixed, something at rest in the universal whirl: *God, Beauty, Truth.*" Ruth Sager, a Woods Hole biologist and friend, wrote that doing science is "much like being an artist or a dancer" (Pardee, 2001). An equally common motivation is to *help people and society*. Biographies abound with stories of those who choose medicine and/or biomedical research to alleviate disease-caused human pain and suffering—often after a personal experience with a loved one. My grandson Luke told me, "I have figured out that there are two professions that help people directly, rather than indirectly: teaching and medicine. I like science so I am going to choose medicine." It is hard to find a scientist who does not love to *solve challenging problems*. These can be as grandiose as those of Steven Weinberg, physicist, who seeks to understand "the rules that govern all phenomena" or as discrete as mine was to unlock a particular molecular configuration. The urge to *satisfy curiosity* is, of course, a driving motivation for scientists, as well as for original inquirers in other fields. Some express curiosity about everything, while others pick a particular phenomenon.

Curiosity governs the choices of artists, of lawyers and of the plumber who finds and fixes the leak. So what is special about doing science? The motivation *to leave something lasting to society and humanity* does fit science particularly well, but so does it fit architects, sculptors and authors. Following in the steps of a mentor is another motivation that fits all disciplines. And, finally, let us not forget the universal motivation for self-preservation: a *search for societal and economic recognition and reward*, an ambition common in virtually all fields. A widely shared ambition to be recognized, to amount to something, such as Jonas Salk seeing a medical degree as a way out of the ghetto, can be found everywhere. And always, motivation must include, for most of us today, making a living, being able to support a family: a job. An ambition often cited for science is well expressed by Edward Neville da Costa Andrade, a physicist, when he was Head Britain's of Royal Institution in the early 1950s. He wrote that the scientific achievement of one generation represents something "won from nature which remains as definite gain and definite progress: an experiment properly carried out remains for all time." The history of science is replete with experiments whose design is memorably "for all time." But the evidence such experiments revealed may not last "for all time" as new and more powerful tools are invented, reveal valid new evidence and demonstrate that human curiosity appears to have no end.

Scientists work alone or in groups, in a laboratory or under the ocean, in caves or in spaceships. Their choices may be influenced by how a mentor, a superior, a key professor chooses to work, as well as by personal and cultural needs, interests and values . . . and simply by what is available to them. The effect of a single laboratory or project head can have enduring influence, extending widely over time, as students of students feel the effects of the judgments of their teachers. There are group as well as individual styles of work. Medawar describes "collectors, classifiers and those that compulsively tidy up" (Medawar, 1979). He also writes of poet-scientists, philosopher-scientists "and even a few mystics." Some are detectives and some are explorers, some artists and some artisans. Immanuel Kant described two kinds of scientists, one looking for unities, the other for heterogeneity and diversity. Later, Hans Christian Oerstod differentiated between those seeking synthesis and others analysis. In the early twentieth century, Wilhelm Ostwald distinguished between "classicists," working "slowly and often morbidly," and "romanticists," working quickly and with enthusiasm. Others have distinguished between the "rationalist," the "empiricist," and the "systemic" processing of scientific facts (Buchdahl, 1993). Another study identifies eight types: the zealot, the initiator, the diagnostician, the scholar, the artificer, the esthetician, the methodologist, and the independent. Sherry Turkle and Seymour Papert describe "canons in scientific thought" as related to cognitive processes (Turkle and Papert, 1991). They consider abstract, formal and logical as the privileged canon of science and hierarchy, and abstraction as the canon of structured computer programmers. Husband and wife teams have worked together in science since its beginnings—at least since Antoine-Laurent and Marie Anne Lavoisier's eighteenth century collaborations. Berta Scharrer delighted in her lifetime endeavor of working with her husband in neuroscience, particularly because "we had the territory practically to ourselves for a long time" (Scharrer, 1987). Margaret Mead said she chose science because it is an activity "where any individual, by finding his own level, can make a contribution." She expressed belief in "many kinds of giftedness" that can make contributions to society through science (Mead, 1972).

If all these choices are open to scientists, we can now add the option of *play*, whose processes are now attracting cognitive study. Scientists often describe their work as play, and Robert Root-Bernstein (1988) highlights how many scientists have incorporated play into their lives and work. We also have these memorable words of Isaac Newton (Brewster, 1855): "I do not know what I may appear to the world, but to myself I seem to have been only like a boy playing on the seashore, diverting myself in now and then finding a smoother pebble or a prettier shell than ordinary, while the great ocean of truth lay all undiscovered before me." Today, the New York Hall of Science uses the mantra "Design, Make, Play" in planning its rich activities and exhibits to engage young and old in science. To this litany of personal and group styles, add national habits, such as Britain's "tea-time," that provide a playtime for "insightful suggestions and broader viewpoints through conversations and collegial interactions with colleagues" (Finn, 2001). How well I remember the very positive influence of the laboratory culture promoted by Professor Irwin Sizer at MIT in the 1940s and 1950s.

But, with all this agreement, there is something on which all scientists do not agree: the power and limits of science. Some believe that scientific knowledge is humanity's highest purpose and thus that there should be no attempt to limit or direct its search for knowledge. At the other extreme, some believe that there are even higher values than the acquisition of knowledge, and thus that science should join with other forms of knowledge in supporting such values. Half a century ago, the science philosopher Karl Popper (1963) addressed the presumptions of science when he suggested that its practice could be encompassed by three doctrines that he described as "culturally established beliefs about the purposes of scientific inquiry":

1. The scientist aims at finding a true theory or description of the world, which shall be an explanation of the observable facts. (This is the doctrine Popper personally supported.)

2. The scientist can succeed in establishing the truth of such theories beyond all reasonable doubt.

3. The best, the truly scientific theories, describe the "essences" or the "essential natures" of the realities that lie behind experiences.

Those who believe that science's power is limited to explaining natural phenomena tend to support equal opportunity for all modes of human inquiry and exhibit collaborative rather than autocratic scientific styles. From Albert Einstein to Rachel Carson, most modern scientists whose writings I have read fit into this category (as do the experiences documented in this memoir), while also leaving room for respect for those with other beliefs . . . i.e., until falsified by further investigation! Those who believe that science can answer questions not just about phenomena, but also about the "essence" of things, tend to value science's mode of inquiry above all others, and believe human reason can solve all problems. Edward Teller and Jonas Salk are examples of those who express this view, and there is plenty of room for others between doctrines #1 and #2!

Talking with students about these doctrines, I learned that most believe Einstein's beliefs would fit under Doctrine #3. On the contrary, Einstein's writings reveal his comfort with Doctrine #1. I well recall Erwin Schrödinger's visit to MIT while I was a graduate student and discussion of his readable slim 1944 volume *What is Life?* Rereading this volume today, I find him telling us that there are inherent limits to scientific inquiry. He writes that science cannot study the ego or the spirit, because all knowledge relates to, indeed exists within, our spirit and our ego. Many other voices are raised to say that science and the spirit, scientific and spiritual values, are compatible, not competitive. Post World II, Vannevar Bush, who set the direction of U.S. governmental policy for the sciences and engineering for decades, stated that "pondering" science should be separated from "pondering" spiritual values. He decries "the extreme materialistic view" and suggests that "to pursue science rightly is to furnish a framework on which the spirit may rise." (Bush, 1967) How well I remember the Doctrine #1 "faith" I expressed in science in my testimonies in Washington, DC.

Do these diverse presumptions of science matter? They matter profoundly when the personal beliefs, tastes and styles of an individual, or a like-minded group of scientists, influence decisions on advancement of students, promotion of faculty, allocation of resources, school and college curricula and presentations to the public. For example, Gerald Holton (1999) documented how careers are influenced by differences between male and female perceptions of "good" science. To Margaret Mead and Rachel Carson, "good" science would include "the human dimension," integrating with the humanities. Isidor Rabi (1960) and James Conant (1945), coming from entirely different disciplines (physics and chemistry), would agree. To Frederick Seitz (2000), as to Jonas Salk (1983), also from very different specialties, "good" science is the most perfectly rational. Dimasio (1994) would be happy for the scientist to be concerned with moral and spiritual issues, while others would not, or would feel it does not matter. Those engaged in the new sciences of complexity would want to add awareness of "emergent" properties and the influence of scale on human behavior.

These varied ideas help us conclude that a full range of different human personal perspectives can be found among scientists. Diversity of perspectives, style and culture can all add value to their results as can other modes of inquiry (artistic, historic, mathematical, technological). The work of scientists is unified by the kind of evidence they pay attention to in drawing their conclusions. My argument for advancing women in science is that diverse perspectives and diverse questions can, unquestionably, add value to an investigation's outcomes. Scientific inquiry is already used by all citizens in cooking, in fixing car engines and in the new world of algorithms, and by all other professionals in their inquiries. Why not use science more broadly and wisely, welcoming it into the panoply of all human inquiry? It can add confidence and competence in problem-solving to all everyday lives, while contributing its unique capacity for useful information about how the world works to all humanity.

At the end of this lifelong litany of voices about and for science, I return to the voices of science teachers. Teaching and learning science are what all my stories have been about. One year in the late 1990s, I kept a record of the answers my New York City secondary science-teacher students gave me when I asked, "Why study science? Why should science be in the secondary school curriculum?" Enrolled in the graduate science education courses I was teaching, they were surprised by the question, but accustomed to satisfying the vagaries of their faculty, they replied. Happily, I decided to write down their answers, and thus I have a record of their responses. They said science "develops the mind and the imagination," "reduces bewilderment about nature," provides a "citizenry with wide-awake minds" and "personal contact with achievement," removes the "cloud of unknowingness," "reduces susceptibility to myth and superstition" and more. They also talked about the usefulness of science: "It sets rules for finding truth, and provides testable answers to big questions." "Lacking a useful understanding of science will lead to exclusion from the mainstream of modern society." "It teaches how to conserve and be healthy," helps "cure diseases" and "find a job in the future," and "assists the U.S. in international competition."

Turning to science in personal life, I asked whether their knowledge of optics added to or subtracted from the beauty they saw in a rainbow, or whether their biological knowledge of the form and function of the human body helped in their daily lives. The class fell silent, finding the answer so obvious that they could not understand my asking it. Then, one after another, they eloquently described how the science they knew enhanced their delight in all they do and see. As one said, "Knowing the source of a rainbow's color makes it even more beautiful to me," and another, "I cannot imagine dealing with everyday life without my knowing some biology of food, health and the environment." Apparently, they agreed with Jonas Salk (1983): "The poet Keats said that science unweaves the rainbow. I find the unweaving just as beautiful, beautiful in a different way."

What a spectrum of personal and practical delights these science teachers find in one academic subject! They believe science should be studied because it is useful and beautiful, good for the nation and good for you. They know that science students have job opportunities not open to others and that the national economy cannot grow without them. And they know the joy and satisfaction gained by individual students when their curiosity is valued and fulfilled. They want their teaching to bring *all* these delights to students. And for them, and for me, engaging in such work makes for a life worth living.

References for Chapters 9 and 10

Born, M. (1936) *The Restless Universe*, Harper and Brothers.

Brewster, D. (1855) *Memoirs of the Life, Writings, and Discoveries of Sir Isaac Newton.* Volume II, Chapter 27.

Buchdahl, H.A. (1993) Styles of scientific thinking. *Science and Education* 2:149–167.

Bush, V. (1967) *Science is Not Enough.* William Morrow & Co.

Conant, J.B. (1945) *General Education in a Free Society.* Harvard Unversity Press.

da Costa Andrade, E.N. (1952) *Science: A Course of Selected Reading by Authorities.* Nottingham, England, International University Society.

Dimasio, A.R. (1994) *Descartes' Error: Emotion, Reason, and the Human Brain.* New York, Avon Books.

Einstein, A. (1934) *The World as I See It.* New York, Covici, Friede.

Finn, J.T. (2001) "British Science: A toast to teatime." *Science* 293(5535):1,589.

Gough, H.G., and D.G. Woodworth. (1960) Stylistic variations among professional research scientists. *The Journal of Psychology Interdisciplinary and Applied* 49(1):87–98.

Holton, G. (1999) Different perceptions of "good science" and their effects on careers. *Annals of the New York Academy of Sciences* 869:78–86.

Jacob, F. (1988) *The Statue Within: An Autobiography.* New York, Basic Books.

Mead, M. (1972) *Blackberry Winter: My Earlier Years.* New York, Morrow.

Medawar, P. (1974). *The Hope of Progress: A Scientist Looks at Problems in Philosophy, Literature and Science.* Wildwood House, London.

Medawar, P.B. (1979) *Advice to a Young Scientist.* New York, Harper and Rowe.

Meselson, M., and F.W. Stahl. (1958) The replication of DNA in *Escherichia coli. Proceedings of the National Academy of Sciences of the United States of America* 44:671–682.

Pardee, A.B. (2001) *Ruth Sager, 1918–1997: A Biographical Memoir.* Washington, DC, The National Academy Press.

Polanyi, M. (1962) *The Republic of Science: Its Political and Economic Theory.* New York, Roosevelt University.

Popper, K. (1963) *Conjectures and Refutations: The Growth of Scientific Knowledge.* London, Routledge & Kegan Paul Ltd.

Rabi, I.I. (1960) *My Life and Times as a Physicist.* Claremont, CA, Claremont College.

Root-Bernstein, R. (1988). Setting the stage for discovery: Breakthroughs depend on more than luck. *The Sciences* May/June: 26–34.

Salk, J. (1983) *Anatomy of Reality*. New York, Columbia University Press.

Scharrer, B. (1987) Neurosecretion: Beginnings and new directions in neuropeptide research. *Annual Review of Neuroscience* 10:1–17.

Schrödinger, E. (1944) *The Physical Aspect of the Living Cell*. New York, Macmillan.

Seitz, F. (2000) *The Miraculous Development of the Scientific Method: A Historical Review*.

Turkle, S., and S. Papert. (1991) Epistemological pluralism and the revaluation of the concrete. Chapter in *Constructionism*, I. Harel and S. Papert, eds, Ablex Publishing Corporation.

Weinberg, S. (2002) Is the universe a computer? *New York Times Review of Books*: 43.

CECILY CANNAN SELBY

Following an A.B. in physics from Radcliffe College and a Ph.D. in physical biology from MIT, Dr. Selby was a research biophysicist at the Sloan-Kettering Institute and Cornell Medical College, engaged in electron microscopic studies of biological cells. After her three sons were born, she moved to educational and administrative work as head-mistress of the Lenox School and National Executive Director of Girl Scouts of the U.S.A., was President of Americans for Energy Independence, and served as director of several for-profit corporations and nonprofit institutions.

Returning to science through science education, she helped found, as dean, the North Carolina School of Science and Mathematics, and was appointed co-chair of the National Science Board's 1983 Commission, "Educating Americans for the Twenty-First Century." This work led to her continuing and primary commitment to the professional development of science teachers, a professorship in science education at New York University and trusteeship (now Trustee Emerita) of the NY Hall of Science.

SELECTED PUBLICATIONS BY THE AUTHOR

The Lotmar-Picken" X-ray diffraction diagram of muscle. With R.S. Bear, *Nature*, 1951.

Microscopy. II. Electron microscopy: A review. *Cancer Research*, 1953.

An electron microscope study of thin sections of human skin. *Journal of Investigative Dermatology*, 1957.

Better performance from "nonprofits." *Harvard Business Review*, 1978.

Managing "volunteers" and their organizations. *Chemtech*, 1980.

Science as "the fourth R—basic and also beautiful! *Science Digest*, Sept. 1980, pp. 44-47.

Science education: Some strategies for success. *The Chemist*, 1982.

Turning people on to science. Editorial, *Physics Today*, July 1982, p. 96.

Trust and tradition: Evolution and entropy. Guest Editorial, *NAIS*, 1982.

Educating Americans for the Twenty-First Century: A Plan of Action for Improving Mathematics, Science and Technology Education for All American Elementary and Secondary Students so that Their Achievement Is the Best in the World by 1995. 1983. Co-author of report of the National Science Board Commission on Precollege Education in Mathematics, Science and Technology, National Science Foundation.

Current trends in mathematics, science, and technology education: Implications for technology innovation. Chapter in *Technological Innovation for the 80's*, James S. Coles, editor, Prentice-Hall, 1984.

Technological literacy: A national imperative and benefit. *Bulletin of Science, Technology & Society*, 1986.

Integrated mathematics, science and technology education. *The Technology Teacher*, 1988.

Technology: From myths to realities. *Phi Delta Kappan*, May 1993.

Outcomes-based education. *The Science Teacher*, October 1993.

Changing the rules: Women in science and engineering. *Radcliffe Quarterly*, Fall 1998.

Women in science and engineering: Choices for success. Cecily Cannan Selby, editor, *Annals of the New York Academy of Sciences #869*, 1999.

A century of women scientists. *Radcliffe Quarterly*, Winter 2000.

Shifting the agenda: From the needs of women to the needs of science. *Bulletin of Science, Technology and Society* 23(1), 2003.

The missing person in science. *The New York Academy of Sciences Magazine,* May/June 2006.

What makes it science? A modern look at scientific inquiry. *Journal of College Science Teaching,* July 2006.

Is science bias holding back women? *FASEB Journal,* July 2006.

33344638R00110

Made in the USA
Middletown, DE
14 January 2019